Chicken, The Way Grandma Liked It

Say Goodbye to Boring Chicken with 300 Recipes for Easy Dinners, Braises, Wings, Stir-Fries, and So Much More

- Christie T. Knutson -

ORIENTAL CHICKEN TENDERS CURRIED PEANUT CHICKEN	9
ORIENTAL CHICKEN WINGS	10
APRICOT CHICKEN WINGS	10
CHICKEN WINGS	11
HOT-N-SPICY CHICKEN WINGS	11
CHICKEN BITS	11
SPICY CHICKEN WINGS	12
CHICKEN FRY ICED TEA	12
TERIYAKI CHICKEN WINGS	13
HOT CHICKEN WINGS	13
HIDDEN VALLEY CHICKEN DRUMMIES	14
MARINATED CHICKEN WINGS	14
GOLDEN CHICKEN NUGGETS	14
MARINATED CHICKEN WINGS	15
SWEET AND SOUR CHICKEN WINGS	15
CHICKEN WINGS IN SOY SAUCE	16
BUFFALO-STYLE CHICKEN WINGS	16
CRISPY CASHEW CHICKEN (MADE IN WOK)	17
CURRIED CHICKEN BALLS	17
LIGHT CHICKEN SALAD	18
HOT CHICKEN SALAD	18
CHICKEN AND ALMOND SALAD	19
CHICKEN SALAD	19
CHICKEN SALAD SUPREME	19
CHICKEN SOUP WITH TINY MEATBALLS	20
CHICKEN TORTELLINI SOUP	21
SEASONING MIX FOR CHICKEN	21
MARINADE FOR CHICKEN	22
CHINESE CHICKEN SALAD DRESSING	22
CHICKEN CASSEROLE	23
CHICKEN DIVAN	23
CHICKEN DIVAN	24
CHICKEN POT PIE	24
CHICKEN WITH RICE	25
CHICKEN TIKKA	25
HONEY SPICED CAJUN CHICKEN	26
ITALIAN CHICKEN	26
LEMON - PARSLEY CHICKEN BREASTS	27
MARY'S CHICKEN DISH	27
NO - PEEK SKILLET CHICKEN	28
QUICK CHICKEN	28
SWEET & SOUR CHICKEN	28
CHICKEN CACCIATORE	29
SUNDAY FRIED CHICKEN	29

HONEY BAKED CHICKEN	30
BAKED CHICKEN	30
BAKED CHICKEN BREASTS	31
SICILIAN CHICKEN	31
ROAST CHICKEN WITH ALMONDS	32
WALDORF CHICKEN	32
CHICKEN A LA KING	33
ORIENTAL CHICKEN	33
CHICKEN YUM YUM!	33
CHICKEN IN ORANGE SAUCE	34
CHICKEN AND RICE	34
CHICKEN PIPLAF	34
POTTED CHICKEN WITH PEPPERS AND MUSHROOMS	35
CORDON BLEU	35
MARINATED CHICKEN	36
CHICKEN KABOBS	36
RUSSIAN CHICKEN	37
TURKEY DIVAN	37
CHICKEN WALNUT	37
SCALLOPED CHICKEN	38
APRICOT CHICKEN	38
BOWL OF THE WIFE OF KIT CARSON	39
CHICKEN A LA WORCESTERSHIRE WINE SAUCE	39
CHICKEN ALMOND CASSEROLE	40
CHICKEN AND BROCCOLI WITH RICE	40
CHICKEN AND DUMPLINGS	41
CHICKEN AND RICE ALMONDINE SQUASH	41
CHICKEN BREASTS IN SOUR CREAM	42
CHICKEN IN SOUR CREAM GRAVY	43
CHICKEN BREASTS IN SOUR CREAM WITH MUSHROOMS	43
CHICKEN BREAST WITH HONEY - WINE SAUCE	43
CHICKEN CASSEROLE	44
CHICKEN CASSEROLE	44
CHICKEN CHARDONNAY	45
CHICKEN CURRY	45
CHICKEN ENCHILADAS	46
CHICKEN FRIED RICE	46
CHICKEN PECAN QUICHE	47
CHICKEN SARONNO	48
CHICKEN ST. STEVENS	49
CHICKEN WELLINGTON	49
CHICKEN WITH NESTS	50
CHUNKY CHICKEN CASSEROLE	50
CONTINENTAL CHICKEN	50
CREAMY HAM AND CHICKEN MEDLEY	51

EASY CHICKEN TETRAZZINI	51
THE EYES OF TEXAS SAUSAGE CHICKEN CASSEROLE	52
FRAN'S CHICKEN	53
GREAT AND EASY CHICKEN CASSEROLE	53
GREEK LEMON CHICKEN	53
GRILLED CHICKEN WITH FLORIDA BARBEQUE SAUCE	54
LEMON CHICKEN SAUTE	55
LUNCHEON CHICKEN CASSEROLE	55
MARINATED CHICKEN BREASTS	56
MARINATED CHICKEN SANDWICHES	56
MOCK CHICKEN KIEV	57
OVEN FRIED CHICKEN	57
OVERNIGHT CHICKEN DIVAN	58
POTATO CHIP CHICKEN	58
RALPH AND RADINE'S FAVORITE CHICKEN SPAGHETTI	59
RANCHER'S SUNDAY CHICKEN	59
RHONDA'S MARINATED CHICKEN SAUCE	60
CAJUN TURKEY BURGERS	60
WINE CHICKEN	60
CHICKEN TURNOVERS	61
CHICKEN POT PIE	61
MOZZARELLA CHICKEN	62
BAKED CHICKEN PARMESAN	62
BAKED CHICKEN SALAD	62
BAKED CHICKEN SALAD	63
BARBECUE CHICKEN	63
BRANDIED CHICKEN BREAST	64
CAROLYN'S CHICKEN & RICE	64
CHICKEN & ANDOUILLE SMOKED SAUSAGE GUMBO	64
CHICKEN BREAST EDEN ISLE	65
CHICKEN - BROCCOLI CASSEROLE	66
CHICKEN CASSEROLE	66
CHICKEN CASSOULET	67
CHICKEN CHOPSTICK	67
CHICKEN DIVAN CASSEROLE	68
CHICKEN DIABLE	68
CHICKEN ELIZABETH	68
CHICKEN ENCHILADAS	69
CHICKEN ENCHILADA CASSEROLE	69
CHICKEN LASAGNE	70
CHICKEN MACARONI CASSEROLE	70
CHICKEN ROYALE	71
CHICKEN SALAD CASSEROLE	71
CHICKEN SHISH - KA - BOBS	72
CHICKEN & SHRIMP CASSEROLE	72

CHICKEN POT PIE	73
CHICKEN PIE	73
DOUBLE CRUST CHICKEN POT PIE	74
CRISPY MUSTARD CHICKEN	74
FRAN'S CHICKEN CASSEROLE	75
ITALIAN ROAST CHICKEN	75
OVEN FRIED CHICKEN BREASTS	76
PINEAPPLE CHICKEN	76
PRESBYTERIAN CHICKEN CASSEROLE	77
SKILLET HERB ROASTED CHICKEN	77
SOUR CREAM CHICKEN CASSEROLE	78
MAXINE'S CHICKEN TETRAZZINI	78
CHICKEN TETRAZZINI	78
SWEET AND SOUR CHICKEN	79
PAELLA	79
HERBED – TURKEY or CHICKEN - IN - A – BAG	80
SOUTHWEST TURKEY or CHICKEN BURGERS	80
COUNTRYSTYLE CHICKEN	81
CASSEROLE CHICKEN	81
CHICKEN POT PIE	81
CHICKEN NOODLE CASSEROLE	82
BAKED CHICKEN	82
ORIENTAL CHICKEN	83
CHICKEN CASSEROLE	83
HONEY GLAZED CHICKEN (LOWFAT)	84
PINEAPPLE GLAZED CHICKEN	84
CHICKEN BROCCOLI VEGETABLE SAUTE	84
20-MINUTE CHICKEN PARMESAN	85
GARLIC CHICKEN	85
SAUTEED CHICKEN	86
BAKED CHICKEN AND RICE	86
NO PEEK CHICKEN	86
CHICKEN AND ZITI CASSEROLE	87
CHICKEN DIVINE	87
CHICKEN BREASTS IN CREAM SAUCE	88
ITALIAN CHICKEN WITH FRESH VEGETABLES	88
CHICKEN AND WILD RICE	89
CHICKEN BREASTS	89
CHICKEN PARISIENNE	89
CHICKEN CASSEROLE	90
CHICKEN AND RICE DINNER	90
CRUNCHY CHICKEN CASSEROLE	91
CHICKEN IN THE GARDEN	91
CHICKEN NOODLE CASSEROLE	91
SWISS CHICKEN	92

Chicken, The Way Grandma Liked It

EASY CHICKEN TETRAZZINI	51
THE EYES OF TEXAS SAUSAGE CHICKEN CASSEROLE	52
FRAN'S CHICKEN	53
GREAT AND EASY CHICKEN CASSEROLE	53
GREEK LEMON CHICKEN	53
GRILLED CHICKEN WITH FLORIDA BARBEQUE SAUCE	54
LEMON CHICKEN SAUTE	55
LUNCHEON CHICKEN CASSEROLE	55
MARINATED CHICKEN BREASTS	56
MARINATED CHICKEN SANDWICHES	56
MOCK CHICKEN KIEV	57
OVEN FRIED CHICKEN	57
OVERNIGHT CHICKEN DIVAN	58
POTATO CHIP CHICKEN	58
RALPH AND RADINE'S FAVORITE CHICKEN SPAGHETTI	59
RANCHER'S SUNDAY CHICKEN	59
RHONDA'S MARINATED CHICKEN SAUCE	60
CAJUN TURKEY BURGERS	60
WINE CHICKEN	60
CHICKEN TURNOVERS	61
CHICKEN POT PIE	61
MOZZARELLA CHICKEN	62
BAKED CHICKEN PARMESAN	62
BAKED CHICKEN SALAD	62
BAKED CHICKEN SALAD	63
BARBECUE CHICKEN	63
BRANDIED CHICKEN BREAST	64
CAROLYN'S CHICKEN & RICE	64
CHICKEN & ANDOUILLE SMOKED SAUSAGE GUMBO	64
CHICKEN BREAST EDEN ISLE	65
CHICKEN - BROCCOLI CASSEROLE	66
CHICKEN CASSEROLE	66
CHICKEN CASSOULET	67
CHICKEN CHOPSTICK	67
CHICKEN DIVAN CASSEROLE	68
CHICKEN DIABLE	68
CHICKEN ELIZABETH	68
CHICKEN ENCHILADAS	69
CHICKEN ENCHILADA CASSEROLE	69
CHICKEN LASAGNE	70
CHICKEN MACARONI CASSEROLE	70
CHICKEN ROYALE	71
CHICKEN SALAD CASSEROLE	71
CHICKEN SHISH - KA - BOBS	72
CHICKEN & SHRIMP CASSEROLE	72

CHICKEN POT PIE	73
CHICKEN PIE	73
DOUBLE CRUST CHICKEN POT PIE	74
CRISPY MUSTARD CHICKEN	74
FRAN'S CHICKEN CASSEROLE	75
ITALIAN ROAST CHICKEN	75
OVEN FRIED CHICKEN BREASTS	76
PINEAPPLE CHICKEN	76
PRESBYTERIAN CHICKEN CASSEROLE	77
SKILLET HERB ROASTED CHICKEN	77
SOUR CREAM CHICKEN CASSEROLE	78
MAXINE'S CHICKEN TETRAZZINI	78
CHICKEN TETRAZZINI	78
SWEET AND SOUR CHICKEN	79
PAELLA	79
HERBED – TURKEY or CHICKEN - IN - A – BAG	80
SOUTHWEST TURKEY or CHICKEN BURGERS	80
COUNTRYSTYLE CHICKEN	81
CASSEROLE CHICKEN	81
CHICKEN POT PIE	81
CHICKEN NOODLE CASSEROLE	82
BAKED CHICKEN	82
ORIENTAL CHICKEN	83
CHICKEN CASSEROLE	83
HONEY GLAZED CHICKEN (LOWFAT)	84
PINEAPPLE GLAZED CHICKEN	84
CHICKEN BROCCOLI VEGETABLE SAUTE	84
20-MINUTE CHICKEN PARMESAN	85
GARLIC CHICKEN	85
SAUTEED CHICKEN	86
BAKED CHICKEN AND RICE	86
NO PEEK CHICKEN	86
CHICKEN AND ZITI CASSEROLE	87
CHICKEN DIVINE	87
CHICKEN BREASTS IN CREAM SAUCE	88
ITALIAN CHICKEN WITH FRESH VEGETABLES	88
CHICKEN AND WILD RICE	89
CHICKEN BREASTS	89
CHICKEN PARISIENNE	89
CHICKEN CASSEROLE	90
CHICKEN AND RICE DINNER	90
CRUNCHY CHICKEN CASSEROLE	91
CHICKEN IN THE GARDEN	91
CHICKEN NOODLE CASSEROLE	91
SWISS CHICKEN	92

SOUTHERN CHICKEN CASSEROLE	92
CHICKEN STIR-FRY FEAST	93
CHICKEN AND NOODLES (HOMEMADE)	93
FRIED CHICKEN BREAST	94
LEMON CHICKEN SAUCE	94
BARBECUE SAUCE FOR CHICKEN	95
MARINATED CHICKEN WINGS	95
LEMON CHICKEN	95
CHICKEN CORDON BLEU	97
NANA'S CHICKEN AND BISCUITS	97
CHEESY TOMATO BASIL CHICKEN BREASTS	98
CHICKEN BREAST SOUTHWESTERN	99
MARINATED CHICKEN	99
CHICKEN TIDBITS	99
YOGURT CHICKEN PAPRIKA	100
CHICKEN PAPRIKA	100
CHICKEN AND STUFFING	101
SOFT CHICKEN TACOS	101
LOU'S LUCKY CHICKEN AND MACARONI	102
CHICKEN MARSALA ALA DAN GARRIS	102
CITY CHICKEN	102
COUNTRY CHICKEN	103
CHICKEN AND WILD RICE	103
LEMON-TARRAGON CHICKEN	104
CHICKEN IN CHEESE SAUCE	104
CHICKEN BREASTS	105
CHICKEN FINGERS	105
CHICKEN DIVAN	106
QUICK AND EASY CHICKEN MARINADE	106
CHICKEN, VEGETABLE, RICE CASSEROLE	106
BEMA'S CHICKEN AND RICE CASSEROLE	107
CHICKEN CACCIATORE	107
CHICKEN PICCATA	108
ORIENTAL CHICKEN WONTONS	108
CURRY CHICKEN	109
CHICKEN WITH RICE	109
FAJITA - STYLE CHICKEN BREASTS	110
TERIYAKI CHICKEN	110
CHICKEN AND PORK ADOBO	111
APPLE CHICKEN CASSEROLE	111
SAUTEED CHICKEN LIVERS	111
POTTED CHICKEN	112
CHICKEN RICE BAKE	112
TOM'S CHICKEN ENCHILADAS	113
CHICKEN FRIED STEAK	113

ITALIAN CHICKEN	114
SO EASY OVEN - FRIED CHICKEN	114
MEXICAN CHICKEN CASSEROLE	114
CHICKEN POT PIE	115
CHICKEN POT PIE	115
EASY CHICKEN POT PIE	116
SOUR CREAM AND CHICKEN ENCHILADAS	116
THYME CHICKEN	116
CHICKEN CASSEROLE	117
CHICKEN SPAGHETTI	117
CHICKEN SPAGHETTI	118
MOZZARELLA CHICKEN AND SAUCE	118
CHICKEN WITH MOZZARELLA CHEESE	118
SWISS CHEESE CHICKEN CASSEROLE	119
CHICKEN DIVAN	119
CHICKEN AND BROCCOLI CASSEROLE	120
CHICKEN LALA PIE	120
CHICKEN TETRAZZINI	121
CHICKEN AND BISCUITS	121
CHEESE `N CHICKEN ENCHILADAS	122
CHICKEN & RICE CASSEROLE	122
SWEET & SOUR CHICKEN	122
CHICKEN BREAST CASSEROLE	123
CHICKEN AND BROCCOLI CASSEROLE	123
HOT CHICKEN SALAD	124
CHEDDAR CHICKEN	124
CHICKEN CASSEROLE	125
BUSY DAY CHICKEN & RICE	125
FESTIVE CHICKEN	126
CHICKEN CASSEROLE	126
PARMESAN CHICKEN	126
CHICKEN POT PIE	127
CHICKEN CASSEROLE	127
CHICKEN BENGALI	127
CHICKEN SPECTACULAR	128
GOURMET CHICKEN	128
CHICKEN WITH PORT	129
CHICKEN IN WINE SAUCE	129
CHICKEN IN WINE	130
CHICKEN ORIENTAL	130
EASY CHICKEN DISH	130
CHICKEN CUTLETS	131
SAUSAGE - CHICKEN DISH	131
CHICKEN ROLL UPS	131
CHICKEN ALA BELGIQUE	132

EASY BARBECUE CHICKEN	132
OVEN BAKED BARBECUE CHICKEN	132
GINGER PEACHY CHICKEN	133
PECAN CHICKEN WITH DIJON MUSTARD	133
CHICKEN OF PUERTO RICO	134
CHICKEN PARMESAN	134
MOZZARELLA CHICKEN	135
RASPBERRY CHICKEN	135
CHICKEN AND CRAB VALENTINE	136
APRICOT CHICKEN	136
BAKED CHICKEN AND POTATOES	137
CHICKEN CRESCENT ALMONDINE	137
CHICKEN AND DUMPLINGS	138
CHICKEN AND RICE	138
CHICKEN WITH SAGE CORN - BREAD CRUST	139
CHICKEN TERI - YAKI	139
CHINESE STYLE FRIED CHICKEN	140
GLAZED ORANGE CHICKEN	140
HERBED CHICKEN	141
ITALIAN CHICKEN CUTLETS	142
LIGHT CAPITAL CHICKEN	142
NO PEEK CHICKEN	143
SKILLET BARBECUED CHICKEN	144
SUNDAY DINNER CHICKEN	144
TARRAGON CHICKEN	145
TERIYAKI CHICKEN	145
BAKED CHICKEN WINGS	146
EASY CHICKEN POT PIE	146
CHICKEN DELIGHT	147
CHICKEN A LA KING	147

Chicken, The Way Grandma Liked It

ORIENTAL CHICKEN TENDERS CURRIED PEANUT CHICKEN

1 c. soy sauce
1/3 c. sugar
4 tsp. vegetable oil
1 1/2 tsp. ground ginger
1 tsp. five spice powder
2 bunches green onion
16 chicken tenders (approx. 2 lbs.)

Blend soy sauce, sugar, oil, ginger and five spice powder in a large bowl until the sugar dissolves. Stir in green onions. Add chicken tenders to marinade. Turn to coat. Cover chicken and refrigerate overnight. Preheat oven to 350 degrees.

Drain chicken RESERVING MARINADE. Arrange chicken in dish and bake until brown and tender, while basting occasionally with marinade.

Another variation of the same recipe:

4 halves, skinned & boned chicken breasts
2 c. half & half
1 1/2 c. mayonnaise
3 tbsp. mango chutney
2 tbsp. dry sherry
1 tbsp. sherry vinegar
2 tbsp. plus 1 tsp. curry powder
1 tsp. turmeric
2 c. finely chopped salted roasted peanuts

Preheat oven to 350 degrees. Place chicken breasts in a shallow baking dish just large enough to hold them. Pour half and half over them and bake for 30 minutes. Let cool and cut in 1 inch cubes.

Process mayonnaise, chutney, sherry, vinegar, curry powder and turmeric in a blender or food processor. Dip chicken pieces into the curry mayonnaise and roll in the chopped nuts. Refrigerate 30 minutes. Arrange on a serving plate with fancy toothpicks.

ORIENTAL CHICKEN WINGS

6 chicken wings
1 sm. clove garlic
1 scallion
1/4 c. soy sauce
2 tbsp. honey
2 tsp. rice-wine vinegar
1/2 tsp.g rated ginger
1/2 tsp. oriental sesame oil
Pinch of cayenne
1 tsp. sesame seeds
1 tbsp. chopped fresh coriander or parsley

Remove wing tips and cut wings in half at the joint. Mince garlic and scallion. Combine soy sauce, honey, vinegar, garlic, ginger, oil and cayenne in a microwave safe dish. Add wings and turn to coat. Marinate at least 30 minutes, turning twice. Put larger wings at the edge of the dish. Cover with plastic and vent. Microwave on high for 5 minutes.

Rotate plate and cook 5 minutes longer. Transfer wings to a serving plate. Return marinade to oven and cook, partially covered on high for 2 minutes. Pour marinade over wings and turn to coat. Sprinkle with sesame seeds, scallion and coriander. 12 pieces.

APRICOT CHICKEN WINGS

1 pkg. Lipton onion soup
1 jar apricot preserves
1 bottle of clear Russian dressing
2 lbs. chicken wings

Bake chicken wings in oven at 350 degrees until tender (1 hour). Mix together soup mix, preserves and Russian dressing. Pour mixture over chicken wings, coating each piece and serve.

CHICKEN WINGS

36 chicken wings
1 (5 oz.) bottle soy sauce
1 tsp. Dijon mustard
4 tbsp. brown sugar
1/2 tsp. garlic powder

Rinse chicken wings and pat dry. Mix soy sauce, mustard, brown sugar and garlic powder together. Marinate wings in mixture overnight (or about 6 hours). Bake wings on cookie sheet for about 1 hour at 375 degrees. Baste wings occasionally with sauce. Serves 9-12.

HOT-N-SPICY CHICKEN WINGS

5 lbs. bag chicken wings (drumettes)
12 fl. oz. Louisiana Pre Crystal Hot Sauce
1-2 sticks butter

Fry chicken wings until golden brown and drain on paper towel. Mix hot sauce and melted butter and pour into deep pan or crock pot. Add chicken wings to sauce and heat thoroughly.

CHICKEN BITS

Debone 2 whole chicken breasts. Cut in bite-size pieces. Dip in melted butter. Roll in seasoned bread crumbs (Italian seasoning with extra Parmesan cheese added). Put on ungreased cookie sheet. Bake at 350 degrees for 30 minutes. Yields 36 bite-size.

SPICY CHICKEN WINGS

1 lg. can Parmesan cheese
2 tbsp. oregano
4 tbsp. parsley
1 tsp. salt
1 tsp. pepper
1 stick margarine
4-5 lbs. chicken wings

Line cookie sheet with aluminum foil. Melt margarine in small pan. Cut up chicken wings. Discard tips. Mix all dry ingredients in bowl. Dunk chicken wings in margarine and roll in cheese mixture. Place on cookie sheet. Bake in preheated 350-degree oven for 1 hour. Serve warm.

CHICKEN FRY ICED TEA

5 lbs. sugar
4 oz. plus 1 c. instant tea
1 gal. boiling water

Blend until sugar melts; let steep. Use 10 gallon container and add large block of ice and 7 1/2 to 8 gallons cold water. Then pour the strong tea solution into it slowly. Stir well. Triple this recipe should serve 500.

CRISPY ORIENTAL CHICKEN WINGS (MICROWAVE)

1 1/2 lbs. chicken wings, disjointed
1 med. egg
1/2 c. soy sauce
2 tbsp. garlic powder
1/4 tsp. ginger powder
1 med. onion, finely diced
2 c. finely crushed corn flakes

Mix together egg, soy sauce, garlic powder and ginger powder. Set aside. On wax paper, mix together crushed corn flakes and diced onion. Dip each wing in soy sauce mixture, then roll in corn flakes and onion. In glass baking dish, cover and cook wings on high (9) for 20 minutes, or until cooked. Remove covering halfway through cooking. Use 13"x9" baking dish. Yield: 24 appetizers.

TERIYAKI CHICKEN WINGS

1/3 c. lemon juice
1/4 c. soy sauce
1/4 c. vegetable oil
3 tbsp. chili sauce
1 clove garlic, finely chopped
1/4 tsp. pepper
1/4 tsp. celery seed
Dash of dry mustard
3 lb. chicken wings

MARINADE: Combine lemon juice, soy sauce, oil, chili sauce, garlic, pepper, celery seed and mustard. Stir well, set aside. Cut chicken wings at joint and remove wing tips. Place chicken in baking dish.

Pour marinade over chicken. Cover, refrigerate at least 4 hours or overnight. Drain and place on broiler tray. Broil about 10 minutes each side with tray about 7 inches from heating element. Brush occasionally with marinade.

HOT CHICKEN WINGS

Chicken wings
1/2 stick margarine
1 bottle Durkee hot sauce
2 tbsp. honey
10 shakes Tabasco
2 tsp. cayenne pepper (optional)

Deep fry wings for 20 minutes. Drain and dip and let set in sauce. Take out to dry and then serve.

----

300 Chicken Recipes

HIDDEN VALLEY CHICKEN DRUMMIES

20 chicken drummies
Good 1/4 c. butter, melted
1 tbsp. hot pepper sauce
2 tbsp. vinegar
2 pkgs. Hidden Valley dressing mix
Paprika
Celery sticks

Dip chicken in mixture of melted butter, pepper sauce and vinegar. Put in baking pan. Sprinkle with 1 package dry dressing mix. Bake 30 minutes at 350 degrees or until browned. Sprinkle with paprika. Serve with celery sticks and prepared Hidden Valley dressing mix as dip.

MARINATED CHICKEN WINGS

2 doz. chicken wings
5 oz. bottle soy sauce
2 tbsp. brown sugar
1 tsp. Dijon mustard
1/2 tsp. garlic powder

Cut chicken wings in half. Marinate in remaining mixture for 1/2 hour. Bake at 350 degrees for 1 hour or until marinate is thick. Turn once. Serves 6 to 10.
COMMENT: *May be frozen in marinade. Bake after defrosting.*

GOLDEN CHICKEN NUGGETS

4 whole chicken breasts, skinned & deboned
1/2 c. unseasoned fine bread crumbs
1/4 c. grated Parmesan cheese
1 tsp. salt
1 tsp. thyme (or 1/4 tsp. powdered thyme)
1 tsp. basil
1/2 c. butter, melted

Chicken, The Way Grandma Liked It

Cut chicken into bite-size pieces. Mix dry ingredients. Dip chicken into butter, then into crumb mixture. Bake on foil-lined cookie sheet at 400 degrees for 10 minutes. Serves 8 to 10.

MARINATED CHICKEN WINGS

1/2 c. soy sauce
1/2 c. honey
1 tsp. garlic powder
1 tsp. chili powder
2 lb. chicken wings with drum end cut at joint from wing, discard tips

Mix ingredients together and marinate cut-up wings overnight. Place wing parts in shallow baking pan and pour remaining liquid over them. Bake for 1 hour at 325 degrees, turning on the 1/2 hour.

SWEET AND SOUR CHICKEN WINGS

2 1/2 lb. chicken wings with tips   removed
1/3 c. Crisco
1/3 c. vinegar
1/2 c. firmly packed dark brown sugar
1 (12 oz.) can unsweetened pineapple juice
3/4 c. catsup
1 tbsp. soy sauce
1 tsp. prepared mustard
1/8 tsp. salt (optional)

Brown wings in hot Crisco, adding more, if necessary. Remove wings as they brown. Drain drippings from skillet. Add vinegar, sugar, juice, catsup, soy sauce, mustard, and salt to skillet. Bring to boil, stirring occasionally.

Simmer gently about 5 minutes. Add browned chicken wings. Cover skillet. Simmer 15 minutes. Turn wings and cook uncovered 15 minutes longer. Serve with rice. Makes 4 servings.

----

300 Chicken Recipes

CHICKEN WINGS IN SOY SAUCE

24 chicken wings
1 c. soy sauce
3/4 c. chopped green onions with tops
1/3 c. sugar
4 tsp. salad oil
1 clove garlic, crushed
1 1/2 tsp. ground ginger

Halve the wings and throw away the tips. Blend soy sauce, onions, sugar, oil, garlic and ginger in a large bowl.

Add the wings, cover and marinate for 30 minutes. Remove the wings and reserve the marinade. Place the chicken in a shallow pan and baste with the sauce. Bake in 350-degree oven for 15 minutes and turn over, baste again and cook 15 more minutes.

This may be made the day before and reserved in refrigerator, covered. Be sure to save some marinade to baste again when reheating in oven.

BUFFALO-STYLE CHICKEN WINGS

2 1/2 lb. (12-15) chicken wings
1/4 c. Durkee red hot sauce
1 stick (1/2 c.) melted butter or margarine
Celery sticks
Blue cheese dip

Split wings at joint and discard tips. Arrange on a rack in a roasting pan. Cover wing pieces with sauce on both sides. Bake at 425 degrees for 1 hour, turning halfway through cooking time. Wings can be deep fried at 400 degrees for about 12 minutes and then dipped into the hot sauce until coated completely. Serve with celery and blue cheese dip.

Chicken, The Way Grandma Liked It

CRISPY CASHEW CHICKEN (MADE IN WOK)

2 egg whites
1 1/4 c. finely chopped cashew nuts
2 whole chicken breasts, skinned, boned and thinly sliced
2 c. peanut or vegetable oil
1/4 c. cornstarch
1 tsp. sugar
2 tsp. salt
1 1/2 tbsp. dry sherry

In small bowl, combine cornstarch, salt, sugar and sherry. In separate bowl, beat egg white lightly until just frothy. Gradually add cornstarch mixture. Stir gently until blended. Place chopped cashews on plate. Dip chicken slices into egg mixture, then coat with cashews. Place on waxed paper. Pour oil into wok, place tempura rack onto wok, making sure rack is level and hooks rest securely on edge of wok. Heat oil over medium to medium-high heat until it reaches 375 degrees. Drop 5 or 6 slices of chicken carefully into hot oil, using a slotted spoon. Fry until golden brown, about 2 to 3 minutes. Remove from oil and place on tempura rack to drain and keep warm.

Continue frying remaining chicken pieces. Makes about 32 appetizers.

CURRIED CHICKEN BALLS

2 (3 oz.) pkg. cream cheese, softened
2 tbsp. orange marmalade
2 tsp. curry powder
3/4 tsp. salt
1/4 tsp. pepper
3 c. finely minced cooked chicken
3 tbsp. minced green onion
3 tbsp. minced celery
1 c. finely chopped almonds, toasted

In a mixing bowl, combine first 5 ingredients. Beat until smooth. Stir in chicken, onion and celery. Shape into 1-inch balls; roll in almonds. Cover and chill until firm (can refrigerate up to 2 days). Yield: about 5 dozen appetizers.

LIGHT CHICKEN SALAD

3/4 c. light mayonnaise
1/2 tsp. ginger
1/2 tsp. salt
3 c. cooked chicken
1 1/2 c. red seedless grapes
1 c. sliced celery
1/3 c. sliced green onion
1/2 c. broken walnuts

Combine mayonnaise, ginger and salt. Stir in chicken, grapes, celery, green onion and walnuts. Makes 5 1/2 cups. Serve on lettuce leaf.

HOT CHICKEN SALAD

1 1/2 c. cooked chicken, diced
1 c. diced celery
3 diced boiled eggs
1/2 tsp. salt
1 sm. jar pimentos
2 tbsp. chopped green onions
1 1/2 c. bread crumbs
1/2 c. slivered almonds
3 tbsp. lemon juice
3/4 c. mayonnaise
1 can cream of chicken soup
1 stick oleo

Mix everything together except breadcrumbs, and oleo. Butter casserole dish (10 x 12 inch). Put complete mixture in dish. Put breadcrumbs on top. Melt butter and sprinkle over the breadcrumbs. Bake at 350 degrees for 30 minutes or until breadcrumbs are brown.

CHICKEN AND ALMOND SALAD

1 1/2 c. cooked chicken
3/4 c. diced celery
1 1/2 tbsp. lemon juice
1/2 c. seedless white grapes
1/2 c. almonds
1/2 tsp. dries mustard
3/4 tsp. salt
1/16 tsp. pepper
1/8 c. light cream
1 hard boiled egg, sliced
1/2 c. mayonnaise

Mix cream and mayonnaise together with mustard, lemon juice, salt and pepper. Pour over other ingredients. Delicious!

CHICKEN SALAD

1 can chicken, chopped (or 5 oz. cooked chicken)
1/2 c. chopped celery
1/3 c. chopped sweet pickle
1 boiled egg, chopped
1/2 c. salad dressing

Mix and serve.

CHICKEN SALAD SUPREME

2 lg. chickens (3 to 4 lb. each to make 6 to 8 c. cooked meat)
4 tbsp. salad oil
4 tbsp. orange juice
4 tbsp. vinegar
2 tsp. salt
3 c. mandarin oranges
2 c. pineapple chunks
3 c. green grapes

Slivered almonds
3 c. diced celery
2 1/2 c. raw rice
1 qt. mayonnaise

Cut chicken into pieces and boil until tender with no seasonings. Remove skin and fat first. Remove meat from bones and cut into cubes. Mix together oil, orange juice, vinegar, salt, marinate chicken in this mixture in refrigerator overnight. Drain fruit well, add to nuts and celery the next day; add to chicken mixture. Cook rice until tender in boiling water, drain, blanch with cold water, drain well; add to chicken mixture. Add mayonnaise, mix well. Serve with crackers and lettuce or in pocket bread.

CHICKEN SOUP WITH TINY MEATBALLS

2 lb. stewing chicken
4 c. water
2 1/2 tsp. basil
1/2 lb. sm. onions
1 bay leaf
1 clove garlic
5 carrots, sliced
Parsley and celery leaves

Place chicken in water in large saucepan. Add salt, pepper, basil, bay leaf and garlic. Bring to boil. Lower heat and simmer slowly for 1/2 hour or until chicken is tender. Remove chicken from pan. Cool and carefully skim fat from surface of soup. Bring soup to a boil and add onions, carrots, parsley and celery, simmer gently for 10 minutes.
 --MEATBALLs --

1 c. finely minced beef
1 egg
1 slice crumbly white bread
1/2 tsp. salt
Freshly ground black pepper

Mix beef with egg, bread, salt and pepper. Form into small meatballs, add meatballs to soup and simmer for 35 minutes. Meanwhile, skim and bone the chicken. Cut meat into small pieces. Garnish the soup with chicken and serve.

CHICKEN TORTELLINI SOUP

2 carrots
1 onion
2 garlic cloves
3 cans cream of chicken soup
6 c. water
1 tsp. oregano
1 tsp. basil
1 pkg. boneless chicken breasts, cut into bite-size pieces
1 bag cheese tortellini
2 boxes frozen broccoli

Cook chicken in small amount of oil. While meat cooks, chop vegetables and open cans. Add all of the above ingredients to large kettle except for the tortellini and frozen broccoli. These 2 ingredients you add the last 10 minutes or so before serving so that they are not over cooked. Simmer the other ingredients for an hour or however long you like. Soup tastes great with freshly grated Italian cheese and a loaf of Italian or French bread.

SEASONING MIX FOR CHICKEN

2 1/2 tsp. salt
1 1/2 tsp. paprika
1 tsp. onion powder
3/4 tsp. savory
1/4 tsp. coriander
3/4 tsp. garlic powder
1/2 tsp. black pepper
1/2 tsp. thyme
1/2 tsp. basil, dried crushed sweet

Mix all ingredients well.
Makes 2 tablespoons plus 2 teaspoons.

MARINADE FOR CHICKEN

1/2 c. shoyu
1/4 c. water
1/3 c. salad oil
2 tbsp. dried minced onion
2 tbsp. sesame seeds
1 tbsp. sugar
1 tsp. ground ginger
1/8 tsp. dried red pepper
3/4 tsp. garlic powder

Mix together all the above ingredients. Marinate chicken parts overnight, turning once, or twice to insure complete marinate. Bake in 350-degree oven for 1 hour. If you intend to use a charcoal grill, bake in oven first for 45 minutes and on grill for 15 minutes. Place marinade in a Ziploc bag with chicken parts. This makes turning easier.

CHINESE CHICKEN SALAD DRESSING

2 tsp. sesame oil
2 tbsp. sesame seeds, roasted
2 tbsp. sugar
2 tbsp. mayonnaise
2 tbsp. lemon juice
2 tbsp. oil
2 tbsp. shoyu

Combine all ingredients and mix well. Drizzle over salad just before serving. This is also a good marinade to pour over skinned chicken the night before grilling it.

For the salad, prepare a green salad, with shredded cooked chicken.
Sprinkle top with dry chow mein noodles.

CHICKEN CASSEROLE

6 chicken breasts
2 onions
8 c. water (approximately)
3/4 loaf bread
Celery
Poultry seasoning
2 tbsp. melted butter
1 can cream of mushroom soup
1 can cream of chicken soup
Sharp cheese, sliced

Boil chicken breasts with 1 onion in approximately 8 cups of water until tender. Remove skin and bones and separate into pieces. Save chicken stock. Use 13 x 9 inch pan (sprayed with Pam). Tear small hunks of bread (about 3/4 of a loaf) and lay in bottom of pan. Slice 1 onion thin and lay on top of bread. Sprinkle celery, poultry seasoning on top. Lay chicken pieces on top. Melt margarine and pour over chicken pieces. Combine mushroom soup, cream of chicken soup and pour on top. Cover the top with sharp cheese sliced all over the top. Bake until done.

CHICKEN DIVAN

3 or 4 deboned chicken breasts
2 cans cream of chicken soup
1 tsp. lemon juice
1 c. sharp American cheese, shredded
2 (10 oz.) pkgs. frozen broccoli
1/2 c. soft bread crumbs, mixed with 2 tsp. melted butter
1 c. mayonnaise

Simmer chicken until tender. Cook broccoli in salted water, drain. Arrange broccoli in greased casserole dish. Place halved chicken breasts on top of broccoli. Combine soup, mayonnaise and lemon juice. Pour over chicken.

Sprinkle cheese and bread crumbs on top. Bake at 350 degrees for 25 minutes. Prepare rice or potatoes for 6 people and serve.

CHICKEN DIVAN

1 lb. cooked chicken, no bones
1/2 lb. cooked chopped broccoli
1 c. shredded extra sharp cheddar cheese
1 can cream of mushroom soup
1 c. croutons

Preheat oven to 350 degrees. Mix chicken (bite-size pieces), broccoli, cheese and soup together. Pour into 8 x 11 inch casserole dish. Place croutons on top. Bake at 350 degrees for 1/2 hour or until hot. Serves 6.

CHICKEN POT PIE

3 lb. chicken
1 can French onion soup
1 lg. carrot
1 lg. celery
Flour to thicken gravy
Water
1 double crust

Preheat oven to 400 degrees. Simmer whole chicken in water with carrot and celery until done, 1 1/2 to 2 hours.

Pick meat off and cut into bite-size pieces. Refrigerate chicken and broth separately overnight. Next day, remove fat from broth as well as carrots and celery. Add onion soup and bring to boil. Thicken gravy with flour-water paste. Strain gravy to remove onions. Put chicken in bottom crust. Pour gravy on top. Place top crust and bake at 400 degrees for 30 minutes.

CHICKEN WITH RICE

3 to 3 1/2 lbs. chicken, cut into serving pieces
1/4 c. butter or margarine
1 1/2 c. instant rice
1 (10 1/2 oz.) can condensed cream of chicken soup
1 c. water
1 tsp. instant chicken bouillon crystals or 1 chicken bouillon cube

Preheat skillet (medium heat), uncovered. Add butter or margarine and allow to melt. Place chicken pieces into skillet and brown on both sides. Season with salt and pepper. Remove chicken from skillet. Reduce heat to "simmer" and add rice. Combine soup, water and bouillon. Pour 1/2 mixture over rice. Replace chicken pieces into skillet onto rice. Pour remaining soup mixture over chicken. Cover and simmer, 35 to 40 minutes or until chicken is done. Makes 4 to 6 servings.

CHICKEN TIKKA

5/8 c. yogurt
4 crushed garlic cloves
1 1/2 inch fresh ginger, peeled & chopped
1 sm. onion, grated
1 1/2 tsp. chili powder
1 tbsp. ground coriander
1 tsp. salt
4 chicken breasts, skinned & boned
1 lg. onion, thinly sliced into rings
2 lg. tomatoes, sliced
2 tbsp. coriander leaves

Combine first 7 ingredients and set aside. Cut chicken into 1 inch cubes. Add to marinade, mix well, cover and chill for 6 hours or overnight. Heat broiler. Put chicken on skewers or in broiler pan and broil (or grill) 5 to 8 minutes, turning occasionally until cooked through.

Garnish with onion rings, tomatoes, and coriander leaves and serve. 4 servings.

HONEY SPICED CAJUN CHICKEN

Paul Prudhomynes seafood magic
10 oz. pounded chicken breast
Cooked linguini
3 sliced mushrooms
1 diced tomato
2 tbsp. mustard
4 tbsp. honey
3 oz. cream

Pat the chicken in the seasonings, then in a very hot fry pan; sear the chicken on both sides until it is done. Take chicken, slice, put back in pan with a little oil, the diced tomato and mushrooms for 2 minutes. Add the honey, mustard and cream. Cook for 5 minutes at medium heat. toss in linguini. Serves 2.

ITALIAN CHICKEN

2/3 c. flour
1 tsp. salt
1/2 c. vegetable oil
1 green pepper
1/2 tsp. pepper
1/2 tsp. garlic salt
Sliced onion
1 lg. jar spaghetti sauce
Chicken (boneless) breasts, quartered

Wash chicken. Mix flour, salt, pepper and garlic together. Coat chicken, brown in oil, then drain. Top chicken with peppers and onions (sliced). Add sauce on top. Cover and simmer about 1 hour. Serve with spaghetti.

LEMON - PARSLEY CHICKEN BREASTS

2 whole chicken breasts, boned & skinned
1/3 c. white wine
1/3 c. lemon juice
2 cloves fresh minced garlic
3 tbsp. breadcrumbs
2 tbsp. olive oil
1/4 c. parsley, fresh

In a measuring cup, combine wine, lemon juice and garlic. Pound each breast until 1/4 inch thick and lightly coat with breadcrumbs. Heat olive oil in a large skillet and brown chicken, 5 minutes on each side. Stir wine mixture and pour over chicken in skillet. Sprinkle on parsley and let simmer 5 minutes. Serve with pan juices.

MARY'S CHICKEN DISH

6 pieces boneless breast of chicken
4 tbsp. olive oil
2 tbsp. butter
1 clove garlic
Breadcrumbs
2 eggs
1 bouillon cube
1 can chicken broth
6 slices of Mozzarella cheese

Dip boneless, skinless chicken breast in breadcrumbs and eggs. In a large skillet, heat olive oil, butter, garlic and melt bouillon cube. Make sure to put heat on low so oil doesn't burn. When oil is hot, brown chicken on both sides in oil, increase heat so chicken gets nice and brown on both sides, lower heat and add chicken broth. Simmer until hot. Add Mozzarella cheese to top chicken.

NO - PEEK SKILLET CHICKEN

2 tbsp. olive or vegetable oil
2 1/2 to 3 lb. chicken, cut into serving pieces
1 (14 oz.) can whole tomatoes, peeled, undrained
1 (4 1/2 oz.) jar sliced mushrooms, drained
1 garlic clove, minced
1 env. Lipton Recipe Secrets onion soup mix
Hot cooked noodles

In a 12 inch skillet, heat oil and brown the chicken; drain. Stir in tomatoes, mushrooms and garlic combined with soup mix. Simmer covered for 45 minutes or until chicken is tender. Serve, if desired, over hot noodles. *Lipton Recipe Secrets beef mushroom soup mix would be a delicious substitute in this recipe.

QUICK CHICKEN

1 can cream of mushroom soup
1 can cream of chicken soup
1 c. milk
5 lbs. cut up cooked chicken
1 pt. sour cream
1 pkg. Pepperidge Farm stuffing mix

Mix soups, sour cream and milk. Add chicken. Mix all ingredients and layer in baking dish alternating with stuffing mix. Bake at 350 degrees for 1 hour.

SWEET & SOUR CHICKEN

1 frying chicken, cut up
1 tbsp. melted butter
Dash of salt, pepper, ginger
3 celery stalks
1 can pineapple (chunk)
2 tbsp. brown sugar
3 tbsp. water

1 1/2 tbsp. soy sauce
1 tbsp. vinegar
1 tbsp. cornstarch
1 red pepper (optional)

Rinse chicken, place skin side up in oiled pan. Pour melted butter over chicken. Sprinkle chicken with salt, pepper, ginger, diced celery. Bake chicken at 325 degrees for about 20 minutes. Drain pineapple juice into cup. Blend in brown sugar, water, soy sauce, vinegar, cornstarch. Pour mixture over chicken in pan. Top with pineapple chunks and pepper.

CHICKEN CACCIATORE

1 pkg. chicken
1/4 c. butter
1/2 c. sherry
15 oz. can stewed tomato bits
1 (6 oz.) can mushrooms
1 pkg. Italian dressing mix
1/4 c. chopped green pepper
1 tsp. Italian seasoning
Garlic powder, to taste
Bayleaf

Boil chicken until done. Save water (use this to boil rice in). Cut chicken into tiny squares. Brown in butter and sherry. Add tomatoes, mushrooms, Italian dressing mix, green pepper and other seasonings. Bring to boil and simmer for one hour. Serve over rice.

SUNDAY FRIED CHICKEN

1 whole chicken or any combo of chicken pieces
1 to 2 c. of flour for coating
Salt and pepper to taste
4 tbsp. butter
4 tbsp. Crisco
2 beaten eggs

300 Chicken Recipes

Wash and dry chicken parts. Combine salt, pepper, and flour and coat chicken. Dip each piece in egg mixture and brown each side in hot, melted shortening and butter. Lower heat and cook for about 15 minutes more on each side. Use heavy iron or aluminum frypan if possible.

Remove from pan and drain on paper towels. Pour all but 3 tablespoons of fat from pan and return to heat. Add 3 tablespoons flour to pan and stir with fat until lightly browned. Add 2 cups of milk and some parsley or parsley flakes and cook on medium heat until thick. Put in gravy boat and serve with the chicken that you have arranged on a platter.

HONEY BAKED CHICKEN

3 or 4 lbs. chicken, cut up
1/2 c. margarine, melted
1/2 c. honey
1 tsp. salt
1/4 c. prep. mustard
1 tsp. curry

Pour over chicken. Bake at 350 degrees for 1 1/4 hours. Basting every 15 minutes.

BAKED CHICKEN

1/2 c. ketchup
1/2 c. mayonnaise
3 tbsp. minced onion
Bread crumbs or crushed corn flakes
2 to 2 1/2 cut up chicken

Mix first three ingredients and dip chicken. Coat with crumbs or flakes. Bake on greased pan or roll lined pan.

Bake at 375 degrees for 40 to 45 minutes.

BAKED CHICKEN BREASTS

8 chicken breast halves, skinned
8 slices Swiss cheese
1 can cream of chicken soup
1/3 c. white wine
1 c. Pepperidge herb stuffing mix
1/4 tsp. melted butter or margarine

Put chicken in very lightly greased baking dish. Top with cheese. Combine soup and wine. Spoon over chicken. Sprinkle with stuffing. Drizzle melted butter over chicken. Bake at 350 degrees 45 to 50 minutes. Serves 6 to 8.

Sarah Frederick

SICILIAN CHICKEN

1 tbsp. plus 1 tbsp. saffron ace
1 lg. onion, sliced
1 lg. green pepper, sliced
1/2 c. fresh mushberries, sliced
1 1/2 lbs. boneless chicken cubed
18 oz. can tomato sauce
16 oz. tomatoes, chopped drained
1 tsp. Worcestershire sauce
1 tsp. oregano
1/2 tsp. basil
1/4 tsp. garlic powder
Lite salt and pepper to taste

Heat oil in large nonstick skillet. Add onions green pepper and mushrooms. Cook until slightly tender. Add chicken. Cook, turning chicken frequently until pinkness is gone. Add remaining ingredients.

Cover and simmer for 5 to 10 minutes until heated through. Serve over rice. Makes 4 servings (1 protein, 2 vegetables per serving).

ROAST CHICKEN WITH ALMONDS

10 chicken breast halves
Salt and pepper
1 (5 1/2 oz.) pkg. slivered almonds
1 (10 1/2 oz.) can cream of mushroom soup
1 (10 1/2 oz.) can cream of chicken soup
1/4 to 1/2 c. dry white wine, or water or other liquid
Parmesan cheese

Spread chicken in very lightly greased baking dish. Cover with 2/3 of the almonds. Mix soups with wine. Pour over chicken and almonds. Sprinkle Parmesan cheese on top and then sprinkle remaining almonds over. Bake at 350 degrees for 2 hours uncovered. Serves 8 to 10.

WALDORF CHICKEN

6 chicken breasts, boned and skinned
1 c. unsweetened apple juice
1/4 tsp. ground ginger
1 tbsp. cornstarch
2 c. unpared red apples, chopped
2 stalks celery, sliced
3 tbsp. raisins
1 tbsp. sliced green onion
1 tbsp. lemon juice
1/4 tsp. salt, opt.

Place chicken, 1/2 cup apple juice, and lemon juice, salt and pepper in non stick skillet. Heat to boiling, cover and simmer for 20 minutes or until chicken is tender and done.

Remove chicken. Mix remaining apple juice and cornstarch. Stirring constantly. Add remaining ingredients. Arrange chicken on plate. Top with sauce.

CHICKEN A LA KING

1/4 c. chopped onion
2 tbsp. chopped green pepper
2 tbsp. margarine
1 can cream of chicken soup
1/2 c. milk
1 1/2 c. cooked, cubed, chicken or turkey
2 tbsp. diced pimiento
Dash red pepper

Cook onion and green pepper in butter until tender. Add soup and milk. Add chicken and remaining ingredients. Heat and serve on toast or cooked rice. Serves 4.

ORIENTAL CHICKEN

1 chicken breast, quarter, cut into slivers
1/2 c. onion, sliced
1/2 c. carrots, sliced
1/2 c. mushrooms, sliced
1 tbsp. peanut oil
1 garlic clove
2 tbsp. low, sodium soy sauce

Heat oil in a large skillet or wok. Saute all ingredients except soy sauce over high heat. Stir fry for 13 minutes and lower heat to medium and cook until chicken is cooked through and legs are tender and crisp about 10 minutes. Toss with soy sauce.

CHICKEN YUM YUM!

1/2 pt. sour cream
8 chicken breasts boned
8 slices ham
1 can cream of chicken soup
1 can cream of celery soup
1 can cream of mushroom soup
1/4 c. sherry cooking wine, opt.

Bone chicken, wrap in slice of ham. Mix other ingredients together. Place chicken in baking dish and pour other ingredients over top. Bake about 2 hours at 325 degrees. (Yum Yum!!)

CHICKEN IN ORANGE SAUCE

4 chicken breast halves
1/4 c. flour
Salt and pepper
4 tbsp. margarine
1 1/2 c. orange juice

Coat each half breast with seasoned flour. Melt margarine in pan and saute each side over medium heat until lightly browned. Add orange juice and cover. Cook about 15 to 20 minutes more on reduced heat until done.

Serve over rice, if desired, with the sauce. Serves 4.

CHICKEN AND RICE

3/4 c. rice
2 cans cream of chicken soup
1 pkg. Lipton cup soup cream of chicken
2 c. water
Chicken pieces, about 2 lbs.

Mix rice, soups, water and put in greased 13 x 9 pan. Place chicken pieces on top and cover with foil. Bake at 325 degrees for 90 minutes. Remove foil and let brown 15 to 20 minutes more.

Can be made the day before and refrigerated until you bake it.

CHICKEN PIPLAF

1 1/3 c. Minute Rice

1 envelope onion soup mix
1 can cream of mushroom soup
1 1/2 c. boiling water
4 tbsp. melted butter
Sprinkle pepper and salt
4 pieces chicken

Combine all ingredients in an ovenproof dish. Brush chicken with melted butter and sprinkle with salt and pepper.

Arrange on top of casserole mixture. Cover with aluminum foil and bake 1 hour and 15 minutes until chicken is done. Can be fixed ahead of time, and then baked.

POTTED CHICKEN WITH PEPPERS AND MUSHROOMS

4 chicken breasts
3 green peppers
2 (3 oz.) cans mushrooms
1 lg. onion
4 potatoes
1 tsp. salt
1/2 tsp. pepper
1 1/2 tsp. paprika
Oil for browning
1 c. water

Brown chicken and remove from pot; brown peppers sliced and remove from pot. Brown onions and mushrooms together; add peppers and chicken, plus seasoning and water. Cover and cook on slow flame after first boil, for 2 hours.

Remove chicken, should be soft. Add peeled potatoes in large chunks and cook for additional 15 to 20 minutes until done in gravy.

CORDON BLEU

3 whole chicken breast, split, skinned and boned
3 slices (4 oz.) Swiss cheese, cut in half
3 slices (4 oz.) boiled ham, cut in half
2 tbsp. margarine

300 Chicken Recipes

1 can cream of chicken soup
1/4 c. milk
Chopped parsley

Flatten chicken breast. Top each with 1/2 slice cheese, then ham. Secure with toothpicks. In skillet brown chicken side down in margarine or butter. Stir in soup, milk and cover. Cook over low heat for 20 minutes. Stir now and then. Top with parsley. Serves 6.

MARINATED CHICKEN

1 c. soy sauce
1/3 c. lemon juice
1/4 c. dry sherry or wine
1/4 chopped green onion
1 garlic clove
Pinch of pepper

Combine all ingredients in a glass or ceramic container and mix well. Marinate chicken for 12 to 24 hours then either grill or broil. Makes enough for 4 to 6 pieces of chicken.

CHICKEN KABOBS

3 boneless chicken breasts
2 jars baby juice (Apple or peach juice)
Teriyaki sauce
Fresh garlic crushed
One clove
2 jars baby food peaches

Mix juice, peaches, garlic and teriyaki sauce in 13 x 9 dish. Add enough teriyaki to your taste. Cut chicken in pieces to place on skewer. Put in marinade overnight. Put chicken on skewers. Cook over grill. While cooking baste well with marinade. Serve with vegetables over rice.

RUSSIAN CHICKEN

1 pkg. dry onion soup
8 oz. bottle red Russian dressing
8 oz. jar apricot preserves
Cut up chicken

Place chicken in baking pan. Combine ingredients and pour over chicken. Bake at 350 degrees for 1 hour.

TURKEY DIVAN

1 (10 oz.) pkg. frozen broccoli
4 lg. slices cooked turkey or chicken
1 can cream of chicken or celery soup
1/3 c. milk
1/4 c. Parmesan grated cheese

Cook and drain broccoli. Arrange in 10 x 6 x 2 baking dish. Combine sour and milk. Pour over turkey. Sprinkle with cheese. Bake at 425 degrees oven about 15 to 20 minutes until brown and bubbly. 3 or 4 servings.

CHICKEN WALNUT

1 lb. chicken boned breast
2 tbsp. cornstarch
1/2 tsp. ground ginger
1/4 tsp. garlic powder
1 tsp. sugar
4 oz. bamboo shoots
3 tbsp. soy sauce
1/2 tsp. salt
2 tbsp. butter
2 tbsp. soy sauce
1/4 c. apple juice
1/4 c. apple juice

Combine, cornstarch, ginger, garlic, sugar and salt. Roll chicken in mixture. Brown chicken in butter and combine 2 tablespoons soy sauce, one half-cup water and one-quarter cup apple juice. Pour liquid over browned chicken.

Cover and simmer 20 minutes or until fork tender. Stir once, add bamboo shoots. Combine one quarter cup water, one quarter cup apple juice and 3 tablespoons soy sauce with cornstarch mix. Left over, add to chicken stir until thick. Serve hot garnished with French fried walnuts. Make by heating one half cup or more walnuts in boiling water five minutes. Remove skins, dry and fry until brown.

SCALLOPED CHICKEN

1/2 loaf white bread cubed
1 1/2 c. cracker crumbs, divided
3 c. chicken broth
3 eggs, lightly beaten
1 tsp. salt
3/4 c. diced celery
2 tbsp. chopped onion
3 c. cubed cooked chicken
1 can (8 oz.) sliced mushrooms, drained
1 tbsp. butter or margarine

In a mixing bowl, combine bread cubes and 1 cup cracker crumbs. Stir in broth, eggs, salt, celery, onion, chicken and mushrooms. Spoon into a greased 2 quart casserole. In a saucepan, melt butter, brown remaining cracker crumbs. Sprinkle over casserole. Bake at 350 degrees for 1 hour. Yield: 6 to 8 servings.

APRICOT CHICKEN

3 - 4 lbs. chicken parts
1 (10 oz.) jar apricot preserves
1 (8 oz.) bottle Kraft Creamy French Dressing
1 pkg. Knorr's Onion Soup Mix

Mix ingredients together and pour over chicken. Bake at 350 degrees for 1 hour. Serve with rice.

BOWL OF THE WIFE OF KIT CARSON

4 c. chicken broth
1 (15 oz.) can garbanzo beans, drained
1 c. chicken, cubed and cooked
1 - 2 chipotle peppers, minced, or 1 tsp. dried pepper flakes
Dash Liquid Smoke
1/2 tsp. paprika
1/2 tsp. dried oregano, crushed
1 med. avocado, sliced
1 c. rice, cooked and hot
1 c. monterey jack cheese, cubed

Bring broth to boil; add beans, chicken, chili peppers, Liquid Smoke, paprika and oregano. Cover and simmer 5 to 10 minutes. Add avocado slices. Mound rice and chunks of cheese in soup bowls. Ladle in hot soup. Serves 6.

CHICKEN A LA WORCESTERSHIRE WINE SAUCE

2 tbsp. veg. oil
2 1/2 lb. chicken, cut up
Salt and pepper, to taste
16 baby carrots, peeled, or 2 lg. carrots, peeled and cubed
1 med. red onion, sliced, or 16 pearl onions, peeled
1 green bell pepper, sliced
1 red bell pepper, sliced
16 sm. mushrooms, sliced
3/4 c. Lea and Perrins White Wine Worcestershire Sauce
1/4 c. yogurt or light cream

Heat oil in a large skillet, season chicken and brown pieces over moderately high heat until golden on all sides, about 15 minutes. Add vegetables and turn to glaze. Drain excess fat. Pour white wine worcestershire sauce over all. Cook 15 minutes more, basting occasionally, until chicken and vegetables are tender. Stir in yogurt or cream and warm through. Serves 4.

CHICKEN ALMOND CASSEROLE

1 c. chicken breast, diced and cooked
1 can cream of chicken soup
1 c. sliced almonds
1/2 c. mayonnaise
1 c. celery, chopped
1/2 tsp. salt
1/2 tsp. pepper
1 tsp. lemon juice
3 eggs, hard-boiled
1 c. cracker crumbs (I use Zesta)
2 1/2 tsp. butter

Mix together cracker crumbs and butter; set aside. Combine chicken, chicken soup, almonds, mayonnaise, celery, salt, pepper, eggs and lemon juice. Grease a deep casserole dish and pour mixed ingredients in alternating layers with 3/4 cup of buttered cracker crumbs. Bake at 400 degrees for 20 to 30 minutes or until bubbly. Cover with remaining buttered crumbs and brown. Serves 6.

CHICKEN AND BROCCOLI WITH RICE

1 1/2 c. water
1 1/2 c. Minute Premium long grain rice
1 lb. chicken breasts, boned and cut into strips
2 tbsp. oil
1 (10 3/4 oz.) can cream of chicken soup
1/2 can milk
2 tbsp. Dijon style mustard
1/2 c. cheddar or Swiss cheese, grated
1 1/2 c. broccoli cuts
2 tbsp. pimento, chopped (optional)

Bring water to a boil. Stir in rice. Cover, remove from heat, let stand 5 minutes. Meanwhile, cook and stir chicken in hot oil until lightly browned. Stir in soup, milk, mustard and cheese, Add broccoli and pimento. Bring to a full boil. Reduce heat and simmer 2 minutes. Pour over rice. Serves 4.

CHICKEN AND DUMPLINGS

1 stewing chicken, cut into pieces
4 c. water
3 stalks celery with leaves, cut into chunks
1 carrot, peeled and sliced
1/2 c. onion, coarsely chopped
2 tsp. salt
1/4 tsp. pepper
1/3 c. flour
1 c. milk
2 tsp. parsley, minced
Biscuit dumplings (below)

Combine first seven ingredients in a large covered pot. Bring to a boil. Reduce to a simmer for 2 1/2 hours. Remove chicken to plate. Strain broth, measure and add enough water to make 3 cups liquid. Mix together flour and milk. Return broth to pan and bring to a boil. Stir in flour and milk mixture. Cook until thickened, stirring constantly, and simmer 3 to 5 minutes. Return chicken pieces to gravy and cover. Prepare dumplings. Drop by spoonfuls into gently bubbling gravy. Cover pan and cook 20 to 25 minutes. Before serving, sprinkle with parsley.

--BISCUIT DUMPLINGS--

1/4 c. Crisco
2 c. self-rising flour
1/3 c. milk

Cut Crisco into flour then stir in milk. Drop by spoonfuls into broth. Cover and simmer for 20 minutes.

CHICKEN AND RICE ALMONDINE SQUASH

3 acorn squash, halved
1/2 c. almonds, natural sliced
1/4 c. margarine
2 tbsp. maple syrup
1 c. long grain rice
1 c. chicken broth

1/4 c. raisins
2 tsp. orange peel
2 chicken breasts, cubed
2 tbsp. margarine
Pepper
Garlic powder

Bake squash at 350 degrees for 45 minutes in 1" water. When squash is baked, brush with butter and syrup.

Bake 5 minutes more. Melt 2 tablespoons margarine in skillet and cook chicken slowly. Season with pepper and garlic powder.

Cook rice in chicken broth until done. Add raisins, almonds, orange peel and chicken to rice. Scoop into squash, using squash as a bowl. Serves 6.

CHICKEN BREASTS IN SOUR CREAM

6 chicken breasts, split and boned
2 c. sour cream
1/4 c. lemon juice
2 tsp. salt
4 tsp. worcestershire sauce
3 tsp. garlic salt
1/2 tsp. paprika
1/2 tsp. pepper
1 c. breadcrumbs
1/2 c. margarine, melted
1/2 c. butter, melted

Rinse chicken breasts and pat dry. In bowl, combine sour cream, lemon juice and seasonings. Roll chicken breasts in sour cream mixture, place in bowl and top with any remaining sour cream. Cover; refrigerate overnight. Remove chicken breasts, taking up as much of sour cream mixture as possible. Roll chicken in breadcrumbs to coat well.

Place in baking dish. Mix margarine and butter; pour half the melted butter and margarine over chicken and bake at 350 degrees for 45 minutes. Pour remaining butter sauce over chicken and bake 5 minutes more. Serves 6.

CHICKEN IN SOUR CREAM GRAVY

2 sm. fryer chickens, cut up
Salt and pepper, to taste
1/4 lb. butter or margarine
3 c. milk
2 tbsp. parsley, chopped
1/4 c. sherry
1 1/2 c. sour cream

Season chicken with salt and pepper. Saute in butter until golden brown. Place chicken and drippings in casserole. Cover with milk. Cook very slowly (about 325 to 350 degrees), about 30 minutes or until tender. Add parsley and sherry. Cook 5 to 10 minutes more. Add sour cream & stir into gravy. Keep in oven another 5 minutes or more. Check for doneness.

CHICKEN BREASTS IN SOUR CREAM WITH MUSHROOMS

4 whole chicken breasts, halved
1 (4 oz.) can sliced mushrooms, drained
1 can cream of mushroom soup
1/2 soup can sherry wine
1 c. sour cream
Paprika

Arrange chicken in a shallow baking dish so that pieces do not overlap. Cover with mushrooms. Combine undiluted soup, sherry and sour cream, blending well. Pour over chicken, completely covering it. Dust with paprika. Bake at 350 degrees for 1 1/2 hours. Serves 4.

CHICKEN BREAST WITH HONEY - WINE SAUCE

1 c. dry white wine
4 tbsp. soy sauce
1/4 tsp. garlic powder
4 chicken breasts, skinned, boned and cut into pieces
4 tbsp. veg. oil
1/2 c. honey
1/2 c. flour
1 tsp. salt

1/2 tsp. pepper

In a large bowl, mix the wine, soy sauce and garlic powder. Add the chicken pieces, stir to coat, and marinate for 1 hour in the refrigerator. Drain chicken, reserving marinade. In a shallow dish, mix the flour, salt and pepper.

Lightly dredge chicken, one piece at a time, in the flour. In a large frying pan, heat the oil until moderately hot.

Add chicken and cook, turning, until brown on all sides. Add honey to reserved marinade and pour over chicken.

Cover and simmer for about 15 to 20 minutes or until tender. Transfer chicken to serving platter and spoon sauce over it. Serve over buttered noodles. Serves 4.

CHICKEN CASSEROLE

2 c. chicken, cooked and cut into small pieces
1/4 lb. egg noodles
1 can cream of chicken soup
4 c. Stove Top Stuffing mix
1 stick butter, melted
1/2 c. milk

Butter 1 1/2-quart casserole dish. Cook noodles according to package, drain and pour into dish. Top with cooked chicken and chicken soup. Mix butter with stuffing mix and put on top of soup. Pour milk over the top of casserole. Bake at 350 degrees for 25 minutes. Serves 4 to 6.

CHICKEN CASSEROLE

1 (10 oz.) box Wheat Thins, crushed
2 c. chicken, cooked and diced
1 (15 oz.) can asparagus, cut spears
1 (8 oz.) can water chestnuts, sliced
2 cans cream of chicken soup
1 c. Hellmann's mayonnaise
1 c. cheddar cheese, grated
1 stick butter or margarine

Combine soup and mayonnaise. Place 1/2 of crushed Wheat Thins in the bottom of a 9" x 13" greased baking dish. Place 1/2 of the soup and mayonnaise mixture, then asparagus, mushrooms, diced chicken, water chestnuts and cheddar cheese. Top with remaining soup and mayonnaise mixture.

Melt butter and combine with remaining Wheat Thins. Sprinkle evenly over casserole. Bake at 350 degrees for 35 to 40 minutes, or until hot and bubbly around the edges.

CHICKEN CHARDONNAY

2 (6 oz.) chicken breasts, boned and skinned
2 tbsp. butter
2 tbsp. shallots, chopped
1 c. fresh mushrooms, sliced
1/4 c. chardonnay (or other dry white wine)
1 tbsp. lemon juice
Flour
1 tbsp. veg. oil
1/4 c. heavy cream
Parsley, chopped

Pound chicken flat; set aside. In butter, saute shallots; add mushrooms and saute 2 to 3 minutes. Add wine and lemon juice; let simmer 6 to 7 minutes. Dredge chicken in flour and season if desired. Saute in oil in frying pan.

Add cream to mushroom mixture and heat until reduced. On warm serving plates, place mushrooms over chicken breasts. Sprinkle with chopped parsley and serve immediately.

CHICKEN CURRY

10 chicken drumsticks (or other cuts)
3 med. potatoes
4 tbsp. curry powder (or more if desired)
8 oz. sour cream
2 lg. cooking onions
2" piece fresh ginger
3 cloves garlic

Salt to taste
5 tbsp. cooking oil
1 c. water

Cut the cooking onions, ginger and garlic into smaller pieces. Put them into a food processor and mince finely. Skin and cut potatoes into quarters. Mix the curry powder with some water to make a paste. Heat oil in a non-stick Dutch oven.

Stir-fry the minced onion mixture until fragrant. Add in the curry paste and stir-fry, mixing well for 2 minutes. Add the chicken and potatoes. Mix well. Cook, covered, for about 2 minutes. Add sour cream and water. Mix well. Bring to boil and reduce heat to simmer. Cook, covered, on low heat for about 30 minutes.

Curry tastes best if prepared ahead and served later with hot fluffy rice or a thick wholemeal bread.

CHICKEN ENCHILADAS

6 chicken breasts, halved, cooked and diced
1 med. onion, chopped and sautéed in butter
8 oz. cream cheese, softened
1 sm. can green chilies, chopped
1 pkg. med. flour tortillas
1 can cream of chicken soup
3/4 c. water
8 oz. sour cream
Cheddar cheese, shredded

Combine chicken, onion, cream cheese and chilies. Spoon into flour tortilla and roll up. Place in greased Pyrex baking dish seam side down. Combine soup, water and sour cream. Pour over top of tortillas. Bake in preheated 350-degree oven for 35 to 40 minutes. Sprinkle with cheddar cheese and heat to melt. May be served with rice and beans. May be frozen but omit cheese before freezing. Serves 8 to 10.

CHICKEN FRIED RICE

1 c. chicken, diced and cooked
1 tbsp. soy sauce
1 c. long grain rice, uncooked
1/3 c. salad oil
2 1/2 c. chicken broth
2 1/2 c. onion, coarsely chopped
1/4 c. green pepper, finely chopped

1/4 c. celery, thinly sliced
2 eggs, slightly beaten
1 c. lettuce, finely shredded

Combine chicken, soy sauce and 1/2 teaspoon salt and let stand for 15 minutes. Cook rice in hot oil in skillet over medium heat until golden brown, stirring frequently. Reduce heat and add chicken with soy sauce and broth.

Simmer, covered, for 20 to 25 minutes or until rice is tender. Remove cover for last few minutes. Stir in onion, green pepper and celery.

Cook, uncovered, over medium heat until liquid is absorbed. Push rice mixture to side of skillet and add eggs. Cook until almost set, then blend into rice. Stir in lettuce and serve at once.

CHICKEN PECAN QUICHE

1 c. flour
1 1/2 c. sharp cheddar cheese, shredded
3/4 c. chopped pecans
1/2 tsp. salt
1/4 tsp. coarse pepper
1/3 c. veg. oil
3 eggs, beaten
8 oz. sour cream
1/4 c. mayonnaise
1/2 c. chicken broth
2 c. chicken, cooked and cooled
1/2 c. sharp cheddar cheese, shredded
1/4 c. onion, minced
1/4 tsp. dillweed
1/4 c. pecans, chopped

Combine first five ingredients. Stir in oil and set aside 1/4 of mixture. Put remaining in bottom of 9" pie plate.

Bake 10 minutes at 350 degrees. Combine rest of ingredients and put into crust. Sprinkle remaining 1/4 of mixture on top and bake at 325 degrees for 45 minutes.

CHICKEN SARONNO

6 chicken breasts, boned, skinned and halved
Salt
Pepper
Garlic powder
Curry powder
Flour
1/4 c. butter or margarine
1/2 lb. fresh mushrooms, thickly sliced
1/4 c. Amaretto di Saronno
Grated rind and juice of 1 lemon
1 1/2 c. chicken broth
1 tbsp. cornstarch
Patty shells

Cut chicken into 1" wide strips. Sprinkle with salt, pepper, garlic powder and curry powder. Roll strips in flour. Heat butter or margarine in a large skillet. Brown chicken pieces on all sides. Add mushrooms, Amaretto di Saronno, grated rind and juice. Simmer 5 minutes.

Mix chicken broth and cornstarch. Stir mixture into skillet. Stir over low heat until mixture bubbles and thickens. Season to taste with salt, if necessary. Spoon mixture into patty shell. Garnish with parsley and diced tomato, if desired. Makes 6 servings.

CHICKEN SHERRY

6 chicken breasts, boned
3/4 c. olive oil
1 stick butter or margarine
1/4 bunch parsley
1 onion, chopped
2 c. beef consommé
3/4 c. tomato juice
1/2 c. dry sherry
4 tbsp. flour

Skin breasts, roll and brown in butter and olive oil. Put breasts in roaster. Add flour to oil and butter and add remaining ingredients. Cook a few minutes and pour over chicken in roaster. Cover roaster and bake at 325 to 350 degrees for about 2 hours. If freezing (sauce is better after frozen for a week), bake for only 1/2 hour. Defrost all day when serving, and bake for the remaining 1 1/2 hours at 325 degrees.

CHICKEN ST. STEVENS

4 whole chicken breasts, boned, skinned and halved
8 thin slices Smithfield ham (prosciuto may be substituted)
8 thin slices Swiss cheese
1 can mushroom soup, undiluted
1/2 pt. sour cream
Fresh mushrooms, sliced
1/4 c. sherry or madeira

In a bowl, combine soup, sour cream, wine and mushrooms. Place chicken in a 9" x 13" dish and cover with ham slices. Pour sauce over chicken, reserving a small amount for later. Sprinkle with paprika. Bake, covered, for 45 minutes to 1 hour at 350 degrees. When done, cover with cheese and the remaining sauce. Bake an additional couple minutes until the cheese melts. Serves 8.

CHICKEN WELLINGTON

4 chicken breasts, boned and halved
1 pkg. Uncle Ben's Wild Rice Mix
1 pkg. Pillsbury crescent rolls
1 egg, separated

Cook rice by package directions. Beat egg white and add to rice. Spoon rice onto chicken half. Cover with other half. Separate dough into 4 pieces, using 2 rolls for each piece. Roll each piece with a rolling pin until thin.

Wrap one thin piece of dough around chicken, covering completely. Place chicken in baking pan and brush with egg yolk. Cover pan with foil. Bake at 350 degrees for 30 minutes. Uncover and bake another 20 to 30 minutes until golden brown. Serve with currant sauce (below). Serves 4.

--CURRANT SAUCE--

1 jar red currant jelly
1 tsp. worcestershire sauce
1 tsp. lemon juice
Dash tabasco
1 tsp. dry mustard

Mix together and heat over low heat until melted.

CHICKEN WITH NESTS

8 nested style angel hair pasta
8 chicken breast halves
1 tsp. salt
1/2 tsp. pepper
1 tsp. garlic powder
1 (6 oz.) can sliced mushrooms
1 (10 oz.) pkg. frozen chopped spinach, thawed and drained well
1 (10 3/4 oz.) can cream of chicken soup
2/3 c. water
3 oz. monterey jack cheese, shredded
3 oz. cheddar cheese, shredded

Cook pasta, keeping nest together, about 2 minutes; drain well. Sprinkle salt, pepper and garlic powder over chicken. Put chicken in 9" x 13" pan. Spoon some spinach over each chicken breast. Place pasta nest carefully on top of chicken and spinach. Combine soup and water in pan. Bring to a boil. Mix well and pour over nests evenly. Bake at 375 degrees for 1 hour. Combine cheese and sprinkle over pasta. Bake 5 minutes more. Serves 8.

CHUNKY CHICKEN CASSEROLE

4 chicken breasts, cooked and cut up
2 cans green beans
1 can water chestnuts, sliced
2 cans cream of chicken soup
1 c. mayonnaise
2 tbsp. lemon juice
Cheddar cheese, grated

Mix together soup, mayonnaise and lemon juice. In 9" x 13" pan, layer green beans, chicken, water chestnuts, soup mixture and grated cheese. Bake at 350 degrees for 45 minutes to 1 hour until mixture bubbles.

CONTINENTAL CHICKEN

1 (2 1/4 oz.) pkg. dried beef, rinsed
3 - 4 chicken breasts, halved and boned
6 - 8 slices smoked, lean bacon
1 (10 3/4 oz.) can cream of mushroom soup

1/4 c. sour cream mixed with 1/4 c. flour

Arrange dried beef on bottom of greased crockpot. Wrap each piece of chicken with a strip of bacon and place on top of the dried beef. Mix soup, sour cream and flour together. Pour over chicken. Cover and cook on low 7 to 9 hours (or on high for 3 to 4 hours). Serve over hot buttered noodles or with rice. Serves 6 to 8.

CREAMY HAM AND CHICKEN MEDLEY

1 tbsp. butter
1/2 c. fresh mushrooms, sliced
1/3 c. butter
1/3 c. flour
2 1/2 - 3 c. milk, divided
1 c. Half & Half
1 c. parmesan cheese, freshly grated
1/2 tsp. salt
1/4 tsp. black pepper
1/4 tsp. nutmeg
2 c. chopped cooked chicken
2 c. chopped cooked ham
2 (10 oz.) pkgs. frozen puff pastry shells, baked

Melt 1 tablespoon butter in a large saucepan over medium heat; add mushrooms, and cook until tender, stirring constantly. Remove from saucepan and set aside. Melt 1/3 cup butter in saucepan over low heat; add flour, stirring until smooth. Cook 1 minute, stirring constantly. Gradually add 2 1/2 cups milk; cook over medium heat, stirring constantly, until thickened and bubbly. Stir in whipping cream and next five ingredients. Cook, stirring constantly, until cheese melts and mixture is smooth; stir in chicken and ham. Add enough of remaining 1/2 cup milk for a thinner consistency. To serve, spoon into shells. Yield of sauce is for 10 shells. Note: This can be
made a day ahead and refrigerated. Either microwave or place on the stove to gently warm. May be served over pasta. Serve with a crisp green salad.

EASY CHICKEN TETRAZZINI

1/2 pkg. fine noodles
1 can mushroom soup
1/4 sm. can parmesan cheese

1 (4 oz.) can mushrooms, drained
2 - 3 c. chicken, shredded
1/2 pt. sour cream

Boil noodles in salted water for 8 minutes. Combine noodles, soup, cheese, mushrooms and chicken in a bowl. Stir in sour cream. Place in a greased baking dish and bake at 350 degrees for 30 minutes. Before serving, stir in a bit more cheese.

THE EYES OF TEXAS SAUSAGE CHICKEN CASSEROLE

2 c. chicken, cooked and diced
1 lb. mild pork sausage
1 c. celery, thinly sliced
3 bunches green olives, sliced
1/2 lb. fresh mushrooms, sliced (canned ones can be used)
2 cloves garlic, finely minced
2 cans cream of mushroom soup
2 cans cream of chicken soup
2 - 3 c. chicken broth
1/2 c. wild rice, uncooked
1 c. long grain rice, uncooked
1 tbsp. worcestershire sauce (add to soup mixture)
1/3 c. port wine (add to soup mixture)

Cook the long grain rice according to directions. Cook the wild rice about 45 minutes after washing it well. Drain both rices and mix together. Cook sausage in frying pan until done; drain grease. Combine both soups and then add chicken broth until medium sauce is attained. Saute in small amount of margarine the celery, garlic, onions and

mushrooms until tender crisp. In a large casserole dish, layer the rices, chicken, sausage, vegetables and soup mixture. Top with homemade bread croutons (see below) and bake at 350 degrees for about 45 minutes or until croutons are lightly tanned and casserole is bubbling around the edges.

--HOMEMADE BREAD CROUTONS--

Melt 1/2 cup butter or margarine in pan. Add 3 slices of bread that have been cut into crouton-sized pieces. Stir these together and mix until all pieces are moist with butter. Spread the croutons over the casserole and bake.

(They are worth the added effort.)

FRAN'S CHICKEN

4 whole chicken breasts, skinned and boned
2 cans cream of mushroom soup
1 can milk
16 oz. sour cream
1 sm. bag Pepperidge Farm stuffing

Prepare stuffing according to package directions and let cool. Cook chicken, cut breasts in half and lay in 9" x 13" baking dish. Mix soup, milk and sour cream. Pour over chicken. Sprinkle stuffing over soup mixture. Bake, uncovered, for 1 hour at 350 degrees. Serves 8.

GREAT AND EASY CHICKEN CASSEROLE

2 lg. chicken breasts, halved
1 tbsp. margarine
1 can cream of chicken soup
3/4 c. sauterne wine
1 (5 oz.) can water chestnuts, sliced
1 (3 oz.) can mushrooms
1/4 c. green pepper, chopped

Fry chicken in margarine until golden brown. Remove to baking dish. Combine rest of ingredients and heat in pan for 5 minutes over low heat. Pour sauce over chicken and cover with foil. Bake at 350 degrees for 25 minutes. Uncover and continue cooking for another 25 minutes.

GREEK LEMON CHICKEN

--MARINADE--

1 c. fruity white wine
1/4 c. olive oil
1/4 c. fresh lemon juice

1 tsp. lemon peel, freshly grated
1 tsp. salt
1 tsp. freshly ground black pepper
3 cloves garlic, crushed
----
6 whole lg. chicken breasts, boned and skinned
3 tbsp. olive oil
2 tbsp. butter
2 tbsp. all-purpose flour
1/2 tsp. salt
2 tsp. prepared mustard
1 c. milk
2 egg yolks
Freshly grated peel of 1 lemon
1 tsp. fresh lemon juice
1 tsp. dried dillweed
1/4 c. fresh parsley, minced
1 c. sour cream
1/4 c. butter, melted
1/2 c. feta cheese, crumbled
1 lb. angel hair pasta, cooked al dente and kept warm
1/2 c. muenster cheese, shredded

In a bowl, combine all marinade ingredients. Pound chicken breasts slightly and place in shallow casserole or in plastic Ziploc bags, and cover with marinade. Refrigerate for up to 12 hours. Discard marinade. Heat oil in skillet and saute chicken until tender. Slice and set aside. In saucepan, melt 2 tablespoons butter; blend in flour and salt to create a roux. Add mustard and slowly add milk, stirring constantly until thick and smooth. In small bowl, mix egg yolk, lemon peel and lemon juice together. Whisk a small amount of roux into egg mixture. Then whisk egg mixture into roux and bring to a gentle boil. Remove from heat and add dill and parsley. When parsley wilts, stir in Sour cream. Add 1/4 cup butter, 3/4 cup of the egg sauce and feta cheese to cooked pasta; stir well. Place in greased 9" x 13" casserole and top with sliced chicken, remaining sauce and cheese. Broil until cheese is golden. Serves 6 to 8.

GRILLED CHICKEN WITH FLORIDA BARBEQUE SAUCE

Chicken for grilling
2 sticks butter
1/2 c. cider vinegar
1/2 c. ketchup
2 bottles prepared horseradish (9 oz.)
Juice of 3 lemons, or 1 c. lemon juice

1/2 tsp. salt
1/2 tbsp. worcestershire sauce
1 tsp. hot pepper sauce (optional)

In a stainless steel pot, melt butter slowly. Add vinegar, ketchup, horseradish, lemon juice, salt, worcestershire sauce and pepper sauce. Simmer, uncovered, for 20 to 25 minutes to blend flavors. Use as a basting sauce on chicken. Sauce may be frozen.

LEMON CHICKEN SAUTE

6 chicken breast halves, boned and skinned
3 tbsp. all-purpose flour
Non-stick cooking spray
1/4 c. margarine
1/3 c. teriyaki sauce
3 tbsp. lemon juice
1 tsp. fresh garlic, minced
1/2 tsp. sugar
Rice, cooked

Roll chicken in flour to coat. Spray 10" skillet with non-stick spray. Add margarine and melt. Add chicken breasts. Cook over medium heat until chicken is lightly browned, about 5 to 7 minutes. Turn chicken, cook until lightly browned. Remove chicken and set aside. Stir in teriyaki sauce, lemon juice, garlic and sugar. Return chicken to pan and simmer 3 minutes. Turn chicken and continue cooking until fork-tender, about 2 to 3 minutes. Serve over rice. Serves 4 to 6.

LUNCHEON CHICKEN CASSEROLE

1 1/2 c. chicken, cooked and cut in bite size pieces
1 c. celery, chopped
2 tbsp. onions, minced
3/4 c. mayonnaise
1 1/2 c. rice, cooked
1 can cream of chicken soup
1 c. Special K cereal (or cornflakes, crushed)
1/4 c. almonds
2 tbsp. margarine, melted

Cook rice as directed on box. Drain. Combine celery, onion, chicken, rice, mayonnaise and soup in 2-quart baking dish. Mix well. Mix margarine, almonds and Special K. Top the chicken mixture. Bake, uncovered, at 325 degrees for 30 to 40 minutes.

MARINATED CHICKEN BREASTS

6 very sm. whole chicken breasts, boned, or 3 lg. ones cut in half
3 med. cloves garlic, crushed
1 1/2 tsp. salt
1/2 c. brown sugar, packed
3 tbsp. grainy mustard
1/4 c. cider vinegar
Juice of 1 lime
Juice of 1/2 lg. lemon
6 tbsp. olive oil
Black pepper to taste

Put the chicken breasts in a shallow bowl. Mix garlic, salt, sugar, mustard, vinegar, and lime and lemon juices.

Blend well. Whisk in olive oil and add pepper. Pour over the chicken and refrigerate overnight, covered. Turn over. Remove from the refrigerator 1 hour before you want to cook and let come to room temperature. Grill approximately 4 minutes per side or until done.

MARINATED CHICKEN SANDWICHES

3 cloves garlic, minced
1/2 c. onion, minced
1/2 tsp. ground ginger
1/4 c. + 2 tbsp. white wine vinegar
2 tsp. olive oil
2 tbsp. frozen apple juice concentrate, undiluted
4 (4 oz.) chicken breast halves, skinned and boned
Vegetable cooking spray
4 (2 oz.) whole-wheat rolls, split
1 c. loosely packed, sliced fresh spinach
8 slices tomato

 Combine first six ingredients in a large Ziploc plastic bag. Add chicken. Seal bag. Marinate in refrigerator for 2 hours, turning bag occasionally. Remove chicken from bag, reserving marinade. Coat grill rack with cooking spray; place on grill over medium hot coals. Place chicken on rack and cook 8 minutes on each side, basting frequently with reserved marinade. Remaining items are for the sandwich.

MOCK CHICKEN KIEV

2 whole chicken breasts, skinned, boned and halved
1/2 c. dry breadcrumbs
1/3 c. parmesan cheese
2 tbsp. parsley, minced
1 tsp. salt
Dash pepper
1 clove garlic, minced
1 lemon
Dash paprika
1/2 c. butter or margarine

Blend crumbs, cheese, parsley, salt and pepper. Melt butter and add garlic. Pound chicken a bit if necessary. Dip chicken into garlic butter then crumbs. Coat thoroughly. Roll chicken into light roll, secure with toothpick. Place in baking dish. Squeeze juice of lemon over all. Drizzle any remaining butter over. Bake at 350 degrees for 1 hour.

OVEN FRIED CHICKEN

3 lbs. chicken parts, skinned
6 tbsp. flour
1 tsp. salt
1 1/2 oz. breadcrumbs
1 oz. parmesan cheese
1 egg, beaten
2 tbsp. water

In a bowl, mix flour and salt. In another bowl, mix egg and water. In yet another bowl, mix crumbs and cheese.

Dip chicken in first bowl, then second bowl, then third bowl. Put chicken in 9" x 13" pan sprayed with Pam. Bake 1 hour at 375 degrees.

OVERNIGHT CHICKEN DIVAN

8 chicken breast halves, or 2 lbs. chicken tenders
1 - 2 heads fresh broccoli
1 can light cream of chicken soup, undiluted
1/2 c. fat-free sour cream
1/2 c. light mayonnaise
2 tbsp. dry sherry
1 tsp. paprika
1 tsp. prepared mustard
1/4 tsp. curry powder
1/3 c. parmesan cheese, grated

Cook chicken, preferably by sautéing in one tablespoon of oil. Coarsely chop meat and set aside. Cook broccoli until tender crisp. Arrange broccoli in a lightly greased 9" x 13" x 2" baking dish. Combine soup and next six ingredients (thin if necessary with skim milk); spoon half of sauce over broccoli. Arrange chicken over sauce; top with remaining sauce. Cover and refrigerate up to 24 hours. Bake, uncovered, at 350 degrees for 30 to 35 minutes or until thoroughly heated. Sprinkle with cheese; bake an additional 5 minutes. Yield: 8 servings.

POTATO CHIP CHICKEN

6 chicken breasts, boned
1 bag potato chips, crushed
1 stick butter
1/2 tsp. salt
1/2 tsp. pepper
1/2 tsp. garlic salt
1/2 tsp. onion salt
1/2 tsp. paprika
1 tsp. worcestershire sauce

Preheat oven to 350 degrees. Grease low-sided baking dish. Melt butter and add all ingredients except chicken and potato chips. Dip chicken in butter then roll in potato chips. Place chicken in prepared pan and bake for 45 minutes or until tender. Judie Elliott

----

RALPH AND RADINE'S FAVORITE CHICKEN SPAGHETTI

1 med. chicken, cooked and boned
1 tbsp. margarine
1/2 lg. green pepper, chopped
1 med onion
1/2 lb. fresh mushrooms, sliced, or 1(4 oz.) can mushrooms, sliced
2 cans cream of mushroom soup or cream of chicken soup
2 cans cream of tomato soup
1 can chicken broth
1 (7 oz.) jar green olives, drained
2 tsp. worcestershire sauce
3 drops tabasco sauce
1 tsp. salt
1/4 tsp. pepper
2 (7 oz.) pkgs. spaghetti
5 oz. sharp cheddar cheese, grated

Cook spaghetti according to package directions. Melt margarine in large pan and add green pepper, onion and mushrooms. Sauté until tender. Add the soups, broth, olives, worcestershire sauce and tabasco. Simmer gently for 15 minutes, then add chicken, drained spaghetti and salt and pepper. Remove from heat and add 3/4 of the cheese. DO NOT cook after adding the cheese. Use the remaining cheese by sprinkling it over the spaghetti after pouring it into serving dish.

RANCHER'S SUNDAY CHICKEN

3 lbs. fryer chicken parts
1 c. Hidden Valley Ranch salad dressing, prepared
4 c. cracker or bread crumbs
Salt
Pepper
Paprika

Wash and dry chicken parts. Dip into prepared salad dressing. Spoon crumbs over the dressing to cover. Place in foil-lined pan. Sprinkle with salt, pepper and paprika. Bake, uncovered, at 375 degrees for 1 1/4 hours. Serves 6.

RHONDA'S MARINATED CHICKEN SAUCE

1 c. soy sauce
3 c. water
3 tbsp. dark Karo syrup
1/2 tsp. ground ginger
5 - 6 cloves garlic, minced
1 tsp. worcestershire sauce
4 whole chicken breasts, skinned and boned

Marinate chicken at least 4 hours. Grill on low for 1 hour.

CAJUN TURKEY BURGERS

1 egg, beaten
1 tbsp. worcestershire sauce
1/2 tsp. salt
1/2 tsp. garlic powder
1/2 tsp. onion powder
1/2 tsp. ground red pepper
1/2 c. seasoned fine dry breadcrumbs
1 lb. ground turkey
6 slices bacon

In a large mixing bowl, combine egg, worcestershire sauce, salt, garlic powder, onion powder and red pepper. Add breadcrumbs and turkey; mix well. Shape turkey mixture into six 3/4" thick patties. Wrap a strip of bacon around outside of each patty and fasten with a wooden toothpick. Place patties on the unheated rack of a broiler pan.

Broil 3 to 4" from heat for 15 to 18 minutes or until no pink remains and bacon is done, turning once. Remove toothpicks before serving. Serve in buns and top with tomato slices and chili peppers, if desired. Makes 6 servings.

WINE CHICKEN

1 can cream of chicken soup
1 pkg. onion soup mix
1/2 c. red cooking wine

Put ingredients in heavy pan. Put chicken parts on top. Cover and bake for 1 1/2 to 1 3/4 hours at 350 degrees.

CHICKEN TURNOVERS

1 pkg. refrigerated crescent rolls (8 ct. tube)
2 c. chopped cooked chicken
3 oz. cream cheese, softened
3 tbsp. chopped green onion
2 tbsp. milk
Dash of pepper (optional)
2 tbsp. margarine, melted
2 tbsp. seasoned crumbs

Preheat oven to 350 degrees. In large mixing bowl combine softened cream cheese, milk, pepper, green onion and chopped chicken. Separate rolls into 4 six-inch squares. Spoon 1/4 of the mixture into each square. Bring corners together and seal. Place on ungreased cookie sheet. Brush with melted margarine and sprinkle with seasoned bread crumbs. Bake for 20 to 25 minutes. Serves 4.

CHICKEN POT PIE

2 (10 3/4 oz.) cans cream of potato soup
1 (16 oz.) can or pkg. drained mixed vegetables
2 c. cooked, diced chicken
OR 4 to 5 Market Day chicken steaks, cooked
1/2 c. milk
1/2 tsp. thyme
1/2 tsp. black pepper
2 (9 inch) frozen pie crusts, thawed

Combine first 6 ingredients. Spoon into prepared pie crust. Cover with top crust; crimp edges to seal. Slit top crust. Bake at 375 degrees for 40 minutes. Cool 10 minutes. (6 servings)

MOZZARELLA CHICKEN

4 whole chicken breasts (boneless)
4 eggs
Italian breadcrumbs
3/4 lb. margarine
1/2 lb. fresh mushrooms
1/2 lb. Mozzarella cheese

Slice breasts into serving size pieces. Place chicken in slightly beaten egg for 1 hour. Refrigerate. Sauté mushrooms and set aside. Roll chicken pieces in breadcrumbs and fry in margarine until brown (10 minutes). Place chicken in 9 x 13 dish and put mushrooms on top. Heat oven to 325 degrees. Bake for 10 to 15 minutes. Then add cheese on top. Put chicken back in oven until cheese melts.

BAKED CHICKEN PARMESAN

2 broiler fryers (2 1/2 lb. each) or equivalent pounds in chicken breasts
2 1/4 c. breadcrumbs
2/3 c. Parmesan cheese
3 tbsp. parsley
1 tsp. salt
3/4 c. butter
1 tsp. Dijon mustard
1/2 tsp. Worcestershire
1 sm. garlic clove

Preheat oven to 350 degrees. Rinse chicken and pat dry. Combine crumbs, cheese, parsley and salt. In saucepan, melt butter; beat in mustard, Worcestershire and garlic. Dip chicken in butter, then roll in crumbs. Pat in shallow pan. Bake 1 hour or until golden.

BAKED CHICKEN SALAD

1 can cream of chicken soup
2 c. cooked chicken
3/4 c. mayonnaise
1 tsp. lemon juice
1 c. chopped celery
1/2 sm. onion, diced

1/4 c. chopped pimento
1/2 tsp. pecan or almond, chopped
3 hard boiled eggs, chopped
2 c. crushed potato chips

Mix together all ingredients except potato chips. Top with crushed chips. Bake at 400 degrees for 20 minutes until bubbly.

BAKED CHICKEN SALAD

2 c. cubed chicken
2 c. celery, sliced
1 (10 oz.) pkg. frozen green peas
1/2 c. slivered almonds
2 tbsp. green pepper
1 tbsp. grated onion
2 tbsp. diced pimento
2 tbsp. lemon juice
1/2 tsp. salt
3/4 c. mayonnaise
1 c. grated American cheese

Combine all ingredients thoroughly. Turn into buttered 2-quart casserole. Sprinkle with cheese and bake at 350 degrees for 25 minutes or until cheese is melted. Makes 10 servings and this can be frozen.

BARBECUE CHICKEN

1 bottle Kraft's Russian dressing
1 pkg. Lipton onion soup mix (dry)
1 jar apricot preserves

Pour dressing in bowl. Mix in soup and preserves. Spread over chicken parts. Marinate all day or overnight. Either bake or broil.

BRANDIED CHICKEN BREAST

4 boned & skinned chicken breast
1/3 c. flour
1/2 tsp. salt
Ground pepper
1/4 tsp. tarragon leaves
1/4 c. butter
1/3 c. apricot brandy
3/4 c. chicken broth
1/2 c. sour cream

Mix flour, salt, pepper, tarragon, dredge chicken in flour mixture. Melt butter, fry chicken until browned. Add brandy, flame. Add broth, simmer covered 10 minutes or until done. Add sour cream, warm and serve.

CAROLYN'S CHICKEN & RICE

1 c. cream mushroom soup
1 pkg. dry onion soup mix
1 1/4 cans water
1 c. regular rice, uncooked
4 skinless chicken breasts (can use boneless)

Bake covered for 2 hours at 350 degrees. Put rice on bottom of casserole dish, then lay chicken on top of rice. Pour soup and rice mixture on top. Cover. Good "do ahead".

CHICKEN & ANDOUILLE SMOKED SAUSAGE GUMBO

1 chicken, cut up
Garlic powder
Cayenne pepper
1 c. chopped onion
1 c. chopped bell pepper
1 c. chopped celery
1 1/4 c. flour
1/2 tsp. salt
1/2 tsp. cayenne pepper
Vegetable oil

7 c. chicken stock
1/2 lb. Andoville sausage or Polish kielbasa in 1/4" cubes
1 tsp. minced garlic
2 c. okra (optional)
Hot cooked rice

Remove excess fat from chicken pieces. Rub on garlic powder and cayenne. Let stand 30 minutes. In a bowl combine onions, pepper and celery. Set aside. Combine flour, 1/2 teaspoon salt, 1/2 teaspoon garlic powder and 1/2 teaspoon cayenne in a plastic bag. Add chicken pieces and shake. Reserve 1/2 cup flour. In a heavy skillet heat 1-inch oil to very hot. Fry chicken until brown (5-8 minute side).

Drain on paper towels. Pour cooled oil into glass measuring cup. Scrape pan bottom and return 1/2 cup oil to the pan. Place pan over heat; whisk in remaining 1/2 cup flour.

Cook; whisk constantly until roux is red brown (3-4 minutes). Don't scorch. Remove from heat and add vegetables. Cook until vegetables are soft. Scrape pan bottom. Place stock in large Dutch oven.

Bring to boil. Add roux mixture tablespoons at a time. Reduce heat to simmer; stir in Andoville sausage and minced garlic. Simmer 45 minutes.

Bone cooked chicken; cut meat into 1/2 inch chunks. Stir in chicken. As a main course, serve 1/3 cup rice in soup bowl with 1 1/4 cups gumbo.

CHICKEN BREAST EDEN ISLE

12-14 half chicken breasts, boned
2 jars dried chipped beef
1 (8 oz.) carton sour cream
1 can cream mushroom soup
12-14 slices bacon

Wrap slice bacon around each half breast. Fasten with toothpick. Layer shredded beef on bottom of open pan. Top with breasts.

Cover with mix of soup and sour cream. Bake at 300 degrees, covered with foil for first hour.

Turn to 250 degrees and bake 2 more hours. Baste at halfway time. Remove foil for last 1/2 hour cooking.

Remove toothpicks. A little vermouth or sherry may be added to above, if desired. (For heartier portions, roll 1/2 chicken thigh (boned) inside breast portion

----

CHICKEN - BROCCOLI CASSEROLE

1 can (10 3/4 oz.) cream of mushroom soup
1 can (10 3/4 oz.) cream of celery soup
1 c. mayonnaise or milk
1 tsp. lemon juice
1 bag (20 oz.) frozen broccoli cuts (thawed & drained)
3 lb. (8 c.) cooked chicken (in sm. pieces)
1 c. shredded Cheddar cheese (4 oz.)
1 can (2.8 oz.) French fried onions

Heat oven to 350 degrees. Lightly grease 2 (2 quart) shallow baking dishes. Whisk undiluted soups, mayonnaise and lemon juice in bowl until well blended. Place half broccoli in bottom of each baking dish. Top with half the chicken. Pour soup mixture over each; spread to cover; sprinkle with cheese. Bake 25-30 minutes until lightly

browned. Scatter onions over tops. Bake 5-7 minutes more. To freeze: Cool, wrap tightly in foil and freeze up to 3 months. To reheat frozen, baked wrapped casserole 1 1/2 hours at 350 degrees. Unwrap and bake 10 minutes longer. Chapter KQ, IL Submitted by Colleen Wise

----

CHICKEN CASSEROLE

2 c. cooked diced chicken
1 can water chestnuts
1 can mushrooms
1 can cream of mushroom soup
3/4 c. mayonnaise
1 c. cooked rice
1 c. chopped celery
1/2 c. slivered almonds
1 c. crushed Ritz crackers
Mixed with 1/2 stick melted margarine

Toss all ingredients, except Ritz crackers. Place in 9 x 11 inch casserole. Sprinkle with cracker crumbs. Bake for 45 minutes at 350 degrees. Bubbly and brown. 6-8 servings.

CHICKEN CASSOULET

1 1/2 c. dry navy beans
1 whole med. sized chicken breast, cut into bite-sized pieces
Vegetable cooking spray
4 oz. turkey Polish kielbasa, sliced
2 cloves garlic, minced
1 lg. onion, chopped
1 lg. celery stalk, sliced
3 lg. carrots, sliced
1/4 c. parsley, chopped
1/4 c. dry white wine
1 (8 oz.) can tomato sauce
1 tsp. dried thyme
1 tsp. salt
1/4 tsp. pepper
1 tsp. seasoning salt (optional)
4 c. water

Rinse and sort beans. Cover with 6 cups water and boil 3 minutes. Remove from heat. Cover and let stand 1 hour. Drain and rinse spray. Dutch oven with vegetable cooking spray; add chicken, sausage, garlic, onion and celery. Saute until lightly brown. Add beans, carrots, remaining ingredients and 4 cups water. Simmer about 1 hour, stirring occasionally. Check seasonings. I sometimes add chicken bouillon. Makes 10 cups. Very low calories. About 3 g fat and 35 mg cholesterol. 260 calories.

CHICKEN CHOPSTICK

2 (10 1/2 oz.) cans cream of mushroom soup
1 (3 oz.) can chow mein noodles
1 can or bag cashew nuts
2 c. diced chicken
1/2 c. water
1 1/4 c. celery, cut up
1/4 c. chopped onion
Dash pepper

Combine water and soup; blend. Reserve 1/2 of noodles for top of casserole. Add other noodles to soup mixture with celery, nuts, onion and chicken and toss lightly. Put reserve noodles on top. Bake 20-25 minutes in 375-degree oven.

CHICKEN DIVAN CASSEROLE

4 chicken breasts, boiled & deboned & broken into lg. pieces
1 lg. bunch broccoli, cooked
1 tbsp. lemon juice
1/4 tsp. curry
1 c. mayonnaise
1 can cream of celery soup
1 pkg. shredded Cheddar cheese

Layer chicken pieces on bottom of greased casserole dish. Then broccoli. Mix remaining ingredients and pour on top of chicken and broccoli. Cover with shredded Cheddar cheese. Bake at 350 degrees for approximately 20-30 minutes.

CHICKEN DIABLE

6 chicken breasts
4 tbsp. melted margarine
1/2 c. honey
1/4 c. mustard
1 tsp. salt
1 tsp. curry powder
4 strips well done bacon, crumbled

Bake chicken in 350-degree oven for 30 minutes. Baste with sauce for the last 15 minutes and finally top with crumbled bacon. Serves 6.

CHICKEN ELIZABETH

6 tbsp. butter
8 boneless chicken breast halves
1 pt. sour cream
8 oz. blue cheese

300 Chicken Recipes

1 tbsp. Lea & Perrins
3 crushed garlic cloves
Chopped parsley
White pepper

Preheat oven to 350 degrees. Grease 9 x 13 inch baking dish. Melt butter in large skillet and brown chicken.

Transfer to prepared dish. Combine sour cream, bleu cheese, Lea & Perrins and garlic in bowl. Add white pepper to taste. Spoon over chicken. Bake 45 minutes. Sprinkle with parsley and serve over rice or noodles. Serves 8.

CHICKEN ENCHILADAS

1 chicken (2-3 lb.) cooked & boned
1 med. onion, chopped
1 can cream of mushroom soup
1 can cream of chicken soup
1 c. chicken broth
1 sm. can chopped mild green chilies
1 pkg. corn tortillas (12)
1 lb. long horn cheese, grated
2-3 tbsp. oleo

Brown chopped onion in oleo. Add soups, chicken broth and green chilies. Beat until smooth. Add chopped chicken to sauce. Heat just to boiling. Fill each tortilla with sauce and place in large casserole dish. Top with grated cheese. Bake at 350 degrees for 20-30 minutes or until bubbly. Can be prepared the night before and cooked before serving the next day. Serves 10-12.

CHICKEN ENCHILADA CASSEROLE

1 can boned chicken or 3 chicken breast (cooked)
1 can mushroom soup
1/2 can chopped green chilies
1/4 lb. Cheddar cheese, grated
1/4 lb. longhorn cheese, grated
1 sm. onion, chopped
1 can enchilada sauce
1 pkg. tortillas

Lightly brown chopped onion in oil or margarine. Add chilies, enchilada sauce, soup and chicken. Mix and heat. Place in a greased casserole part of tortillas, then pour a small amount of chicken mixture over them. Cover with grated cheese. Make second and third layers in same manner, with final layer the chicken mixture and topped with cheese. Bake at 350 degrees for 45 minutes. Serves 4.

CHICKEN LASAGNE

8 oz. lasagna noodles
1 can cream of mushroom soup
2/3 c. milk
1/2 tsp. salt
1/2 tsp. poultry seasoning
8 oz. cream cheese, softened
1 c. cream style cottage cheese
1/3 c. chopped onion
1/4 c. minced parsley
3 c. diced cooked chicken
1 1/2 c. soft bread crumbs, buttered
1/3 c. stuffed sliced olives

Cook noodles until tender, drain and rinse. Mix soup, milk, salt and poultry seasoning in a saucepan and heat. Beat cheeses together; then mix in olives, onions and parsley. Place 1/2 in noodles in a buttered 9 x 13 x 2 inch baking dish and spread with 1/2 the cheese mixture, 1/2 the soup mixture and 1/2 the chicken. Repeat layers. Top with crumbs. Bake at 375 degrees for 30 minutes. Let stand 10 minutes before serving. Serves 6-8. Freezes well.

CHICKEN MACARONI CASSEROLE

1 pkg. uncooked creamette macaroni (7 oz.)
1 can cream of mushroom soup
1 can cream of celery soup
1/2 lb. grated Velveeta cheese
15 oz. can water chestnuts
2 c. diced cooked chicken
1/4 c. diced green pepper
1 (2 oz.) jar diced pimentos
1 sm. can mushroom pieces
1 1/2 c. milk
1 tsp. salt

Mix all ingredients in large bowl. Refrigerate overnight. Turn into buttered 9 x 13 inch glass casserole. Bake at 350 degrees for 1 1/4 hours. Tuna, shrimp or crab meat may be substituted for chicken.

CHICKEN ROYALE

4 sm. boneless chicken breasts
1/4 c. flour
1/2 tsp. salt, if desired
1/4 tsp. paprika
Pepper

--STUFFING--

4 c. soft breadcrumbs
2 tbsp. onion
1/2 tsp. salt
1/8 tsp. thyme
Pepper
4 tbsp. melted butter
1/2 c. water

Mix all stuffing ingredients together. Stuff each breast secure with picks, skewers or thread. Put flour, salt, paprika and pepper in paper or plastic bag. Shake each piece of chicken to coat. Slather breasts with melted butter. Bake at 325 degrees for 1 to 1 1/2 hours, turning once. Sprinkle with parsley. Serve with mushroom sauce.

CHICKEN SALAD CASSEROLE

2 c. chopped cooked chicken
1 c. chopped celery
1 can cream of chicken soup
3/4 c. mayonnaise
1 c. sliced diced water chestnuts
1/2 c. slivered almonds
4 tbsp. butter
1 c. crushed corn flakes

Mix all ingredients except butter and corn flakes. Place in ungreased 13 x 9 x 2 inch casserole. Melt butter and mix with corn flakes. Spread over casserole and bake at

350 degrees for 45 minutes. All ingredients may be mixed ahead except corn flakes and butter. This should be put on just before baking. Casserole should be eaten as soon as baked.

CHICKEN SHISH - KA - BOBS

3 lb. chicken, cut in chunks or strips marinade in mixture of
1/3 c. teriyaki sauce
2 tbsp. vegetable oil
2 tbsp. chili sauce
1/4 c. honey
1 tsp. salt
1/2 tsp. ground ginger
1/4 tsp. garlic powder

Alternate chicken on skewers with cherry tomatoes, mushrooms, pineapples, chunked green peppers, chunked onions. Grill and enjoy.

CHICKEN & SHRIMP CASSEROLE

1/2 c. flour
1 lg. frying chicken, cut into serving pieces
1 onion, diced
1 clove garlic
1 can tomato sauce
1 tsp. salt
1/2 tsp. pepper
1 tsp. basil
2 tsp. parsley
1 tsp. paprika
1 can minced clams
1/2 lb. mushrooms, sliced
1/4 c. sherry
1/2 lb. shrimp, peeled & deveined

Dredge chicken in flour. Brown lightly in skillet. Place in casserole. Saute onion lightly. Add garlic, tomato sauce, salt, pepper, basil, parsley, paprika, clams with liquid, mushrooms and sherry. Simmer 10 minutes. Pour sauce over chicken. Cover and bake at 350 degrees for 1 hour. When ready to serve, uncover casserole and add shrimp. Cover shrimp with sauce and bake 10 minutes more at 350 degrees. Serves 6. Can be served over rice.

CHICKEN POT PIE

3 cans white meat chicken, drained
1 can Veg-All, drained
1 can cream of potato soup
1 can cream of mushroom soup
1/2 c. milk or 1/2 c. cooking sherry
Salt & pepper
2 Pillsbury pie crusts
1 egg, for egg wash

Place 1 crust in bottom of 9 inch pie pan. Use egg wash on crust. Mix chicken, Veg-All, soup, milk or sherry, salt and pepper. Place in crust. Top with other crust; seal. Use egg wash and then make slits. Bake at 350 degrees for 40 minutes.

Do not put on cookie sheet.

CHICKEN PIE

1 chicken, boiled & boned
1 can cream chicken soup
1 1/2 c. chicken broth
1 c. flour
1 tsp. baking powder
1/2 tsp. salt
1 tsp. pepper
1 c. milk
1 stick oleo, melted

Combine chicken, soup and broth. Place in 9 x 13 inch dish. Make batter by combining remaining ingredients.

Pour over chicken mixture. Bake at 425 degrees for 30 minutes.

DOUBLE CRUST CHICKEN POT PIE

2 (9") refrigerated pie crusts
1 (6 3/4 oz.) can boneless chicken in broth, undrained & chopped
1 (16 oz.) can mixed vegetables, drained
1 (10 3/4 oz.) can cream of chicken soup, undiluted
1/4 tsp. pepper
1/4 tsp. poultry seasoning
1/4 tsp. celery flakes

Fit 1 refrigerated pie crust into a 9 inch pie plate, according to package directions (do not bake). Combine chicken and remaining ingredients; spoon into pie crust. Moisten edges of pastry with water; place remaining crust on top. Fold edges under and flute. Cut slits in top. Bake at 400 degrees for 45-50 minutes. Let stand 10 minutes before serving. Yield: One 9-inch pie.

CRISPY MUSTARD CHICKEN

2 tbsp. reduced calorie mayonnaise
2 tbsp. prepared mustard
1/4 c. wheat germ
1/3 c. fine dry bread crumbs
1/2 tsp. ground thyme
1/4 tsp. salt
4 (4 oz.) skinned boned chicken breast halves
Vegetable cooking spray

Combine mayonnaise and mustard in a small bowl; stir well. Combine wheat germ and next 3 ingredients in a shallow bowl. Brush each chicken breast with mustard mixture, dredge in breadcrumb mixture.

Place chicken in a 10 x 6 x 2 inch baking dish that has been coated with cooking spray. Cover and bake at 350 degrees for 40 minutes.

Uncover and bake an additional 20 minutes or until chicken is tender. 4 servings.

FRAN'S CHICKEN CASSEROLE

8 chicken breasts, cooked, cubed
1 pkg. wide noodles
1/4 c. butter, melted
1 can cream of mushroom soup
1 can cream of chicken soup
1 pt. sour cream
1 tbsp. sherry
1/4 c. grated onion
1 tsp. seasoned salt
Paprika, optional

Bake chicken 45 minutes in broth and water. Remove chicken, cool and cube. Cook noodles in broth and water according to package directions, being careful not to overcook. Drain, put in bottom of 13 x 9 x 2 inch greased casserole. Drizzle butter over noodles. Mix all remaining ingredients except chicken. Add chicken on top of noodles; then spread sour cream mixture over all. Sprinkle top with paprika. Bake at 350 degrees for 20-30 minutes or until top is slightly brown and casserole is heated through.

ITALIAN ROAST CHICKEN

1 fryer, cut up & washed
2-3 tbsp. oil (for baking sheet pan)
2-3 cloves garlic
Sage leaves, crumpled
Parsley
Garlic salt
Oregano
Salt
Pepper

Place chicken in oven baking sheet covered with 2-3 tablespoons oil. Dice garlic over chicken pieces. Sprinkle other seasonings over chicken. Bake at 350 degrees for 1 hour approximately.

OVEN FRIED CHICKEN BREASTS

8 skinless, boneless chicken breast halves
1/2 c. plain nonfat yogurt
1/2 box Ritz crackers, crushed into fine crumbs

Dip chicken in yogurt and roll in cracker crumbs. Place chicken in baking dish and bake in 350-degree oven 30 minutes on each side. Makes 8 servings.

PINEAPPLE CHICKEN

2 c. sliced raw chicken breasts (1" strips)
18 pineapple cubes, canned
1 whole green pepper, cut into 1" long thin slices
1 c. sliced raw celery
Salt & pepper to taste

--SWEET AND SOUR SAUCE--

1 c. white vinegar
1 c. apricot nectar
1 c. brown sugar
1 tsp. Worcestershire
1/2 bottle tomato catsup
1 tsp. cornstarch

Prepare sauce first by combining all ingredients except cornstarch. Simmer for 30 minutes. Thicken with cornstarch diluted in a little water. Saute chicken in a little oil (do not brown) and add all other ingredients and stir constantly. Add sweet and sour sauce, salt and pepper to taste.

PRESBYTERIAN CHICKEN CASSEROLE

2 c. chicken, cooked & diced
1 can water chestnuts, drained, sliced
1 can LeSueur peas
1 can cream of chicken soup
1 c. (lite) sour cream
1 tube Ritz crackers, crushed
1 stick oleo, melted
2 tbsp. poppy seeds

Combine chicken, water chestnuts, peas, soup and sour cream. Place in 7 x 11 inch greased casserole. Top with crackers mixed with oleo and poppy seeds. Bake 30 minutes at 350 degrees or until bubbly.

SKILLET HERB ROASTED CHICKEN

4 skinless, boneless chicken breast halves
2 tbsp. all-purpose flour
1/4 tsp. ground sage
1/4 tsp. dried thyme
2 tbsp. margarine
1 (10 3/4 oz.) can cream of chicken soup
1/2 c. water

On waxed paper, combine flour, sage and thyme. Coat chicken lightly with flour mixture. In skillet over medium high heat, in hot margarine, cook chicken 10 minutes or until browned on both sides; push chicken to one side.

Stir in soup and 1/2 cup water, stirring to loosen browned bits. Reduce heat to low. Cover; simmer 5 minutes or until chicken is fork tender. Serve over hot cooked rice. Serves 4.

----

300 Chicken Recipes

SOUR CREAM CHICKEN CASSEROLE

3 c. cooked, diced chicken
1 (8 oz.) bag noodles
1 sm. can mushrooms
2 cans cream of chicken soup
1 (16 oz.) sour cream
8 oz. Swiss cheese

Cook and drain noodles. Combine all ingredients except Swiss cheese. Place in 9 x 13 inch pan; top with Swiss cheese. Bake at 350 degrees for 45 minutes.

MAXINE'S CHICKEN TETRAZZINI

Bake 1 chicken or use several chicken breast, boiled 3 c. chicken, chopped
1/2 c. pimento (4 oz. can)
1/2 c. green pepper, chopped
1 can cream of mushroom soup
1 c. chicken broth or more
1 tsp. salt
1 tsp. pepper
1 lb. Cheddar cheese, mild
8 oz. pkg. spaghetti, cooked

Mix all ingredients except half of cheese. Cover with foil. Bake at 350 degrees for 45 minutes. Remove foil and add remainder of cheese and heat until melted. This is great with a green salad and hot French bread.

CHICKEN TETRAZZINI

5 c. cooked, cubed, boneless chicken breast
2 c. sour cream
7 oz. pkg. skinners ready cut spaghetti
2 cans cream chicken soup, undiluted
8 oz. can mushroom pieces, drained
1 stick oleo, melted

White pepper to taste,1 c. grated (freshly) Parmesan cheese Combine all ingredients except cheese. It is not necessary to cook pasta, provided you put the ingredients together a half a day before baking. Place mix in 13 x 9 inch casserole (greased). Can be frozen. When ready to bake sprinkle cheese over top. Bake at 350 degrees for 25-30 minutes or until bubbly. Serves 12.

SWEET AND SOUR CHICKEN

4 whole chicken breasts, split
4 chicken leg thighs (not split)
1 (18 oz.) jar apricot preserves
1 (8 oz.) bottle Russian dressing
1 env. onion soup mix

Place chicken in large shallow baking dish. Combine remaining ingredients and pour over chicken, trying to coat all pieces. Bake at 350 degrees for 75 minutes. Serve with brown rice and spoon some of the sauce over it. In spite of unusual ingredients, it is delicious.

PAELLA

1/2 lb. shrimp, cleaned (chicken can also be used)
2 garlic cloves, crushed
2 tbsp. butter or margarine
1 tbsp. cornstarch
1 1/4 c. chicken broth
1 can (14 1/2 oz.) chopped tomatoes with liquid
1/2 c. sliced pepperoni
1 pkg. (10 oz.) frozen peas, thawed
1/4 tsp. cayenne pepper
1 1/2 c. dry minute rice
1/8 tsp. saffron

Saute shrimp and garlic in butter until shrimp are pink approx. 2 minutes. Stir in cornstarch, cook 1 minute. Add broth, tomatoes, pepperoni, peas and cayenne pepper. Bring to a full boil, stirring occasionally. Stir in rice and saffron. Cover and remove from heat. Let stand 5 minutes. Fluff with fork. Makes 4 servings.

HERBED – TURKEY or CHICKEN - IN - A – BAG

1 (7-10 lb.) turkey or chicken
2 tbsp. dried parsley
1 tbsp. rubbed sage
1 tsp. marjoram
1 tsp. thyme
1 tsp. savory
1/2 tsp. rosemary
1 tbsp. flour

Rinse turkey and dry. Combine parsley and next 5 ingredients in blender; process 1 minute. Sprinkle cavity and outside of turkey with herb mixture. Shake flour into large cooking bag; place in large roasting dish at least 2 inches deep. Place turkey into bag according to directions.   Insert meat thermometer. Bake at 325 degrees until Thermometer reaches 185 degrees. Remove from oven and slit bag open. Remove turkey and let stand 15 minutes before carving. Serve with dressing. Yield 10-12 servings.

SOUTHWEST TURKEY or CHICKEN BURGERS

1 lb. ground turkey or chicken
Bottled mild salsa
1/2-3/4 lb. mushrooms
1 tbsp. salad oil
1/2 tsp. salt
2 tbsp. mayonnaise
4 Kaiser rolls or hamburger buns

In bowl, mix ground turkey or chicken and 1/4 cup salsa; shape into 4 patties. Broil or grill until they lose their pink color turning once. Meanwhile, slice mushrooms. In skillet over medium heat, in hot salad oil, cook mushrooms and salt until lightly browned, stirring frequently. In small bowl mix mayonnaise and 1/3 cup salsa. To serve, cut each roll in half. Spread mayonnaise mixture on bottom halves of buns. Top with patties and mushrooms.

COUNTRYSTYLE CHICKEN

Chicken
Onion
Oil
Allspice
Bay leaf
Salt
Pepper

Brown chicken in small amount oil with onion, add seasoning and spice, cook slow turning often so it won't stick or burn until done.

CASSEROLE CHICKEN

1 whole chicken, cut up
1 (8 oz.) sour cream
1 (10 3/4 oz.) can cream of mushroom soup
1 pkg. dry onion soup mix
1 (3 oz.) can chow mein noodles

Cut chicken into serving pieces - place in a casserole large enough to hold chicken comfortably. Combine sour cream, mushroom soup and onion soup mix. Spread the soup mixture over chicken. Cover with chow mein noodles and bake at 325 degrees for 1 1/2 hours.

CHICKEN POT PIE

2 (10 3/4 oz.) cans cream of broccoli soup
1 c. milk
1/4 tsp. thyme leaves, crushed
1/4 tsp. pepper
4 c. cooked cut up vegetables (broccoli, carrots, potatoes, etc.)
2 c. cubed cooked chicken or turkey

1 (10 oz.) can Hungry Jack flaky biscuits 1. In 3 quart baking dish, combine soup, milk, thyme and pepper. Stir in vegetables and chicken. 2. Bake at 400 degrees for 15 minutes or until mixture begins to bubble.

Meanwhile, cut each biscuit into quarters. 3. Remove dish from oven; stir. Arrange biscuit pieces over hot chicken mixture. Bake 15 minutes or until biscuits are golden brown.

CHICKEN NOODLE CASSEROLE

1 can cream of chicken soup
1/2 c. milk
1 pkg. Meullers dumpling noodles (serve 6)
1 (6 oz. or so) can chicken

Cook noodles per package directions. Add chicken, soup and milk. Simmer for 15 minutes and serve hot.

Additions and substitutions - tuna instead of chicken; cream of mushroom soup instead of cream of chicken; peas, corn or your favorite vegetable.

BAKED CHICKEN

Use 9 x 12 inch pan. 1/2 stick butter
1 onion, sliced thin
1 chicken (may use 2)
1 can mushrooms
1 can cream of chicken soup
1 can cream of celery soup
1 can cream of mushroom soup
Paprika

Dot butter on chickens - add onions, mushrooms - mix soups together - pour over all - sprinkle with paprika. Bake 1 hour at 375 degrees.

ORIENTAL CHICKEN

1/2 c. butter
1/2 c. flour
1 tbsp. salt
1 c. cream
3 c. milk
2 c. chicken stock
2 c. cubed chicken
1/2 c. sauteed sliced mushrooms
1/2 c. blanched almonds
1 c. sliced water chestnuts
1/4 c. pimento strips
1/4 c. sherry

Melt butter in top of double boiler, add flour and salt, cook until bubbly - add cream, milk and chicken stock, stirring until smooth. Cook over hot water for 30 minutes. Just before serving, add the remaining ingredients and heat thoroughly. Serve over souffle, rice, or cheese shell.

CHICKEN CASSEROLE

2 chicken breasts, cooked and shredded
1 bag Pepperidge Farm herb dressing
2 cans chicken noodle soup
1 can cream of chicken soup
3 eggs, beaten
1/2 stick butter or margarine, melted

Butter 9 x 13 inch cake pan. Mix 3/4 bag dressing, chicken, soups and eggs. Put in dish. Drizzle with butter and sprinkle with remaining dressing. Bake at 325 degrees for about 40 minutes.

HONEY GLAZED CHICKEN (LOWFAT)

1 tbsp. ginger
1/4 c. low-sodium soy sauce
1/2 c. sherry
3 tbsp. finely chopped onion
1 1/2 tbsp. honey
5-6 boneless, skinless chicken breasts

Mix together ginger, soy sauce, sherry, onion and honey. Pour on one side of chicken and broil 5 minutes. Turn and pour remaining ingredients on other side of chicken. Broil for 3-5 minutes longer.

PINEAPPLE GLAZED CHICKEN

4 chicken breasts, skinned and deboned
1 (15 oz.) can chunk pineapple
Scallions to top the meat
Salt and pepper
2 tbsp. margarine
1/4 c. packed brown sugar

Salt and pepper chicken breasts, brown in margarine over medium heat. When brown add pineapple and sugar.

Continue cooking until liquid is thickened and forms a sauce. Serve - scant scallions over meat.

CHICKEN BROCCOLI VEGETABLE SAUTE

2 tbsp. margarine, divided
4 skinless, boneless chicken breast halves (about 1 lb.)
1 c. cut-up broccoli
1/2 c. thinly sliced carrots
1 c. sliced mushrooms
1 can Campbell's cream of broccoli soup
1/3 c. milk
1/8 tsp. pepper

In skillet over medium heat, in 1 tablespoon hot margarine, cook chicken 10 minutes or until browned on both sides. Remove chicken; keep warm. In same skillet, in remaining margarine, cook broccoli, carrots and mushrooms 5 minutes, stirring often. Stir in soup, milk and pepper. Heat to boiling. Return chicken to skillet. Reduce heat to low; simmer 5 minutes or until chicken is fork-tender. 4 servings. Preparation time: 10 minutes. Cooking time: 20 minutes.

20-MINUTE CHICKEN PARMESAN

4 boneless and skinless chicken breast halves (about 1 lb.)
1 egg, slightly beaten
1/2 c. seasoned breadcrumbs
2 tbsp. margarine or butter
1 3/4 c. Prego spaghetti sauce
1/2 c. shredded Mozzarella cheese
1 tbsp. grated Parmesan cheese
1/4 c. chopped fresh parsley

Using palm of hand flatten chicken to even thickness. Dip chicken into egg then into crumbs to coat. In skillet over medium heat, in hot margarine, brown chicken on both sides. Add Prego sauce. Reduce heat. Cover; simmer 10 minutes. Sprinkle with cheeses and parsley. Cover; simmer 5 minutes or until cheese melts. 4 servings.

GARLIC CHICKEN

1 bottle olive oil
2-3 cloves of garlic
Whole chicken, cut up or 5 breasts
6 potatoes, peeled and sliced thin
Salt and pepper

Preheat oven to 450 degrees. Pour olive oil in 13 x 9 inch pan. Add garlic cloves. Bake cloves until they pop. Add sliced potatoes and chicken pieces. Lower oven to 400 degrees and bake 45 minutes. Turn chicken after 30 minutes. Season to taste with salt and pepper.

SAUTEED CHICKEN

4 boned skinless chicken breasts
Old Bay seasoning
Olive oil

Sprinkle Old Bay on breasts. Heat olive oil in fry pan - medium heat. Sauté chicken turning often until done, 5-10 minutes.

BAKED CHICKEN AND RICE

1 (10 oz.) pkg. Virgo yellow rice
3 c. boiling water
1 stick margarine or butter, soft
Chicken legs, thighs or breast
Minced or diced onions to taste (optional)

Preheat oven to 350 degrees. Grease oblong dish. Mix rice and margarine or butter. Spread on bottom of greased dish. Add boiling water on top, then lay chicken parts on top. Cover dish with foil and bake 1 hour.

Uncover and sprinkle with paprika (optional) and brown for additional 20 minutes. If you want, you can use 2 cups water "plus" one can of chicken broth.

NO PEEK CHICKEN

1 pkg. Uncle Ben's wild rice
1 can cream of mushroom soup
1 can cream of celery soup
1 soup can of water
1 tsp. parsley
Dash of curry powder
4-6 chicken breasts, boned and skinned
1/2 pkg. Lipton onion soup

Preheat oven to 350 degrees. Grease 9 x 13 inch baking dish. Mix first 6 ingredients; pour into baking dish. Lay chicken breast on top. Sprinkle soup mix over chicken. Cover tightly with foil. Bake 2 1/2 hours. Don't peek until 2 1/2 hours done. Let stand 15-30 minutes before serving.

CHICKEN AND ZITI CASSEROLE

1 jar spaghetti sauce (any variety)
4 c. cooked ziti (6 oz. uncooked)
1 1/2 c. cubed cooked chicken or turkey
1 c. shredded Mozzarella cheese
1 tbsp. grated Parmesan cheese

Use 2 quart casserole - stir together spaghetti sauce, cooked ziti, chicken, and 1/2 cup Mozzarella. Sprinkle with rest of Mozzarella and Parmesan cheese.

Bake at 350 degrees for 30 minutes or until hot and bubbling.

Makes 6 servings.

CHICKEN DIVINE

4 chicken breasts
2 or 3 (10 oz.) boxes frozen broccoli spears, cooked
2 cans cream of chicken soup
1 c. mayonnaise
1/2 tsp. curry powder
1 c. soft bread crumbs (or cracker crumbs)
2 tbsp. melted butter
1 tbsp. lemon juice
4 oz. pkg. shredded cheese

Cook broccoli and arrange in baking dish. Add chicken pieces. Mix soup, mayonnaise, lemon and curry powder.

Pour over chicken. Sprinkle with cheese, crumbs and paprika. Bake 1/2 hour at 350 degrees.

----

300 Chicken Recipes

CHICKEN BREASTS IN CREAM SAUCE

4 chicken breasts halves, boned and skinned and rinsed
1/4 c. flour
1/2 tsp. salt
1/2 tsp. pepper
2 tbsp. butter
2 tbsp. vegetable oil
1/4 lb. mushrooms, sliced
3/4 tbsp. garlic, chopped
1 green onion, chopped

1. Add salt, pepper and flour. 2. Dredge chicken breasts in seasoned flour mix, shake excess off. 3. Add butter and vegetable oil to sauté pan, cook on medium heat. 4. Cook chicken breasts for 2 1/2 minutes on each side. 5. Add mushrooms, garlic - cook for approximately 1 more minute until chicken is almost done, add chopped onion. 6. Drain fat from pan and set aside. Approximately 4 servings.

ITALIAN CHICKEN WITH FRESH VEGETABLES

2 skinless, boneless chicken breast, split
1 (16 oz.) can tomatoes
1 sm. can black olives
1 zucchini, sliced
1 summer squash, sliced
1 green pepper, sliced
Handful of fresh green beans
1 med. onion, cut in wedges
1/2 tsp. oregano
1/4 tsp. basil
Salt and pepper
Garlic powder
Mozzarella cheese, shredded

Season chicken with salt, pepper and garlic powder. Brown chicken in large frying pan. Cover with tomatoes. Cover pan and simmer 20 minutes. Add fresh vegetables and top with oregano and basil - cover pan and continue to simmer for 20 minutes. Add black olives and cover with Mozzarella cheese. Continue to simmer until cheese is melted. Serve over white rice.

CHICKEN AND WILD RICE

1 (6 oz.) pkg. Uncle Ben's wild rice (original)
1 can cream of chicken soup
1 can cream of celery soup
1 can mushrooms
1 whole chicken, cut up
1 pkg. Lipton's onion soup mix

Butter a 13 x 9 inch pan. Mix together rice, soup and mushrooms and spread in bottom of pan. Place chicken pieces on top of rice mixture and sprinkle with onion soup mix. Cover with foil and bake at 350 degrees for about 1 1/2 hours. Serves 4-5.

CHICKEN BREASTS

4 chicken breasts, halved and boned
8 slices Swiss cheese
1/3 pkg. Pepperidge Farm stuffing
1 can cream of chicken soup
1/4 c. milk
1/4 c. margarine

Put chicken breasts, skin side down, in a 9 x 13 inc pan. Lay a slice of cheese on each piece. Dilute soup with milk and divide the mixture equally on each piece. Melt margarine. Mix with dressing and sprinkle on to top. Cover. Bake at 325 degrees for 2 hours. Uncover last 40 minutes.

CHICKEN PARISIENNE

4-6 lg. chicken breasts
1 can condensed cream of mushroom soup
3 oz. (2/3 c.) mushrooms, with liquid
1 c. dairy sour cream
1/2 c. cooking sherry or white wine
Paprika

Place chicken breast in 11 x 7 x 1 1/2 inch baking dish. Combine sour cream, cream of mushroom soup, mushrooms and sherry and pour over chicken. Sprinkle generously with paprika. Bake at 350 degrees about 1 to 1 1/4 hours or until tender. Serve with hot fluffy rice.

CHICKEN CASSEROLE

1 (2-2 1/2 lbs.) chicken, boiled and off bone
1 can cream of mushroom soup
1 can cream of chicken soup
1 (8 oz.) sour cream
1 (8 oz.) Cheez Whiz
1 stick butter or margarine
1 1/2 sleeves of Ritz crackers or saltines
Poppy seeds

Put bite size pieces of chicken in bottom of 9 x 13 inch pan. Mix the soups (undiluted), the sour cream, and the Cheez Whiz together in medium sized bowl. Put this mix on top of chicken. Sprinkle poppy seeds over soup mixture. Melt stick of butter. Crush crackers. Mix together, then sprinkle evenly over chicken casserole. Bake in 350 degree oven for 20-30 minutes, until bubbly and brown. Serves 6. This is a family favorite!

CHICKEN AND RICE DINNER

1 chicken, lg. enough for your whole family
Some butter or margarine
Salt and pepper
Rice - I prefer Uncle Ben's boil-in-bag style (enough for your family)

Wash chicken. Put several pats of butter or margarine on skin. Sprinkle with salt and pepper. Bake in 350 degree oven for approximately 1 hour. Baste chicken after 30 minutes. *Rice* - follow directions on boil-in-bag rice - its quick, easy and delicious. *Gravy* - when chicken is done, remove it from the pan. Heat drippings over medium heat on stove. Thoroughly mix 1/4 cup flour with 1/2 cup of water. Gradually add this to chicken drippings as they boil. You may not need all the flour and water mixture, mix to taste. Boil slowly for 10 minutes on low. Serve hot.

CRUNCHY CHICKEN CASSEROLE

2 cans boned chicken, drained
1 can cream of chicken soup
1 soup can evaporated milk
1 sm. can mushrooms, drained
1 1/4 c. minute rice
1/2 stick margarine, sliced
1/2 c. slivered almonds

Mix and place in casserole dish. Bake 45 minutes at 375 degrees.

CHICKEN IN THE GARDEN

Aluminum foil
Ready to cook chicken pieces
Sm. potatoes
Cherry tomatoes
Med. onions
Fresh mushrooms
Green peppers
Worcestershire sauce
Salt, pepper, paprika
Butter or margarine

Cut off a 40 inch pieces of aluminum foil for each dinner guest. Fold foil in half. Place chicken, potato, tomato, onion, mushrooms, and green pepper on foil. Sprinkle with Worcestershire, salt, pepper and paprika. Dot with butter. Fold foil. Bake in 450 degree oven (in shallow pan) about an hour or cook over glowing coals. Turn package every 20 to 30 minutes.

CHICKEN NOODLE CASSEROLE

1 sm. pkg. egg noodles
1 can cooked chicken, drained

1 can cream of chicken soup
1 soup can milk
Butter
Bread crumbs
Salt and pepper

Cook noodles in boiling water. Drain. Combine soup, milk, chicken, salt and pepper in saucepan. Bring just to a boil. Take off heat and add to noodles in buttered casserole dish. Sprinkle with bread crumbs. Bake in 300 degree oven for approximately 30 minutes or until bubbly and brown.

SWISS CHICKEN

1 stick margarine or butter
1/2 c. milk
10 chicken breast halves, deboned
10 slices Swiss cheese
1 can cream of chicken soup
1 pkg. Pepperidge Farm herb dressing mix (sm.)

Place chicken breast in large flat baking dish. Sprinkle with salt and pepper (salt sparingly). Place 1 slice of cheese on top of each breast. Mix can of soup with 1/2 cup milk and pour over chicken. Melt margarine or butter and mix with dressing mix and spread over chicken. Bake at 325 degrees uncovered for 1 1/2 hours.

SOUTHERN CHICKEN CASSEROLE

1 frying chicken (2 1/2-3 lbs.), cut up
1/2 lb. bacon
4 med. potatoes, pared
1 lg. onion, thinly sliced

1 tsp. poultry seasoning
1 tsp. salt
1/2 tsp. black pepper
1/2 c. chopped shallots, green onions or sliced onions
2 tbsp. chopped fresh parsley

Wash and dry chicken. In Dutch oven, fry bacon until crisp. Remove bacon. Add chicken, browning well on all sides. Remove to a 2 quart casserole dish as pieces brown. Cut potatoes lengthwise into 3 slices. Add bacon fat. Brown on both sides. Remove and place on top of chicken. Top potatoes with onions. Sprinkle with poultry seasonings, salt, pepper, shallots and parsley. Top with bacon , then cover. Bake at 350 degrees for 40 minutes. You may add 2 cups green beans, broccoli, cauliflower or squash. Layer extra vegetables on top of chicken before adding potatoes and onions.

CHICKEN STIR-FRY FEAST

1 c. raw Uncle Ben's original converted brand rice
1 lb. boneless, skinless chicken breasts
3 tbsp. cornstarch, divided
3 tbsp. soy sauce, divided
3 tbsp. dry sherry, divided
1 lg. clove garlic, minced
4 tbsp. peanut oil or safflower oil, divided
1 lg. carrot, julienned
1 lg. green or red bell pepper, cut into strips
1 lg. onion, sliced
1/4 lb. fresh mushrooms, sliced

Cook rice according to package directions. Meanwhile, cut chicken into 1-inch square pieces; combine with mixture of 2 tablespoons cornstarch and 1 tablespoon each soy sauce and sherry, and garlic. Let stand 30 minutes.

Mix remaining cornstarch, sherry and 2/3 cup water; set aside. Heat 2 tablespoons oil in hot wok or large skillet until hot. Add chicken and stir-fry 4 minutes; remove. Heat remaining oil in same pan. Add carrots, bell pepper and onion; stir-fry 4 minutes. Add mushrooms; stir-fry 30 seconds. Stir in chicken and cornstarch mixture. Cook, stirring until sauce boils and thickens. Remove from heat; stir in remaining soy sauce. Serve over rice. Makes 4 servings.

CHICKEN AND NOODLES (HOMEMADE)

4 chicken breasts

Boil chicken until done. Set aside chicken broth. Let breast cool somewhat and then remove meat in pieces. Put pieces of chicken back in broth.

--NOODLES--

1 c. all-purpose flour
1/2 tsp. salt
2 eggs, beaten

Mix flour and salt. Add egg. Turn dough onto a well floured surface. Knead and cover, let stand 30 minutes. Roll dough out onto floured surface, turning dough over and over until paper thin. Allow dough to dry 1 hour, then cut in strips, then allow noodles to dry completely. Add noodles to chicken and cook for about 20 minutes. You can add salt and pepper to taste.

FRIED CHICKEN BREAST

2 Boneless chicken breasts (can also use 1 turkey breast)
1 c. all-purpose flour
1 tbsp. paprika
4 tsp. salt
1/2 tsp. pepper
2 c. bread crumbs
2 eggs
1/2 c. milk

Heat 1 inch salad oil to 370 degrees. Cut chicken into strips. Combine flour, paprika, salt and pepper in bowl - and bread crumbs in another. Mix eggs and milk. Dip chicken in flour mix, then egg mix, then bread crumbs.

Fry a few pieces at a time about 3 to 5 minutes, until tender. Drain on paper towels.

LEMON CHICKEN SAUCE

4 1/2 tbsp. sugar
4 1/2 tbsp. lemon juice
4 1/2 tbsp. chicken stock
3/4 tsp. salt
2 tsp. cornstarch
1 1/2 tsp. sesame oil
1 1/2 tsp. yellow food coloring (optional)
Rind from lemon

Several drops lemon extract

Cook sauce until thick over high heat, stirring constantly. Pour sauce over cooked chicken pieces. Serve hot.

BARBECUE SAUCE FOR CHICKEN

2 c. vinegar
1/2 c. salt
1/2 stick of oleo
1 tsp. hot pepper
1/2 c. water

Cook all ingredients in saucepan until salt is dissolved and to a good rolling boil. Brush over chicken several times during barbecuing.

MARINATED CHICKEN WINGS

3 lbs. chicken wings
1/2 c. soy sauce
1/3 c. salad oil
1 onion, minced
1 tbsp. molasses
4-5 garlic cloves (or sprinkle garlic powder)
1 tsp. dry mustard
1 tsp. Accent

Cut wings in half; cut tip and dispose. Mix all other ingredients and pour over chicken pieces. Marinate 7 to 8 hours in refrigerator, covered. Arrange pieces on cookie sheet and bake, uncovered 1 1/2 hours at 375 degrees. (Turn once after an hour.) Yield: 30 to 40 servings.

LEMON CHICKEN

2 whole chicken
1 tbsp. vegetable oil
1 egg

300 Chicken Recipes

2 tsp. cornstarch
1 tsp. salt
1 tsp. soy sauce (light or dark)
1/4 tsp. white pepper
Vegetable oil
1/4 c. all-purpose flour
1/4 c. water
2 tbsp. cornstarch
2 tbsp. vegetable oil
1/4 tsp. baking soda
1/4 tsp. salt
1/2 c. chicken broth
1/4 c. honey
3 tbsp. lemon juice
2 tbsp. light corn syrup
2 tbsp. vinegar
1 tbsp. vegetable oil
1 tbsp. catsup
1 clove garlic, finely chopped
1/2 tsp. salt
Dash of white pepper
Peel of 1/2 lemon
1 tbsp. cornstarch
1 tbsp. cold water
1/2 lemon, thinly sliced

Remove bones and skin from chicken; cut each breast into fourths. Place chicken in shallow glass or plastic dish. Mix 1 tablespoon vegetable oil, the egg, 2 teaspoons cornstarch, 1 teaspoon salt, the soy sauce, and 1/4 teaspoon white pepper; pour over chicken. Turn chicken to coat both sides. Cover and refrigerate 30 minutes. Remove chicken from marinade; reserve marinade. Heat vegetable oil (1 1/2 inches) in wok to 350 degrees. Mix reserved marinade, the flour, 1/4 cup water, 2 tablespoons cornstarch, 2 tablespoons vegetable oil, the baking soda and 1/4 teaspoon salt. Dip chicken pieces one at a time into batter.

Fry 2 pieces at a time until light brown, 3 minutes. Drain on paper towel. Increase oil temperature to 375 degrees. Fry chicken all at one time until golden brown, turning once, about 2 minutes. Drain on paper towel.

Cut each piece crosswise into 5 or 6 pieces; place in single layer on heated platter. Heat chicken broth, honey, lemon juice, corn syrup, vinegar, 1 tablespoon vegetable oil, catsup, garlic, 1/2 teaspoon salt, dash of white pepper and the lemon peel to boiling. Mix 1 tblsp cornstarch and 1 tblsp water; stir into sauce. Cook and stir until thickened, about 10 seconds. Remove lemon peel. Garnish with lemon slices; pour sauce over chicken. Makes 8 servings.

CHICKEN CORDON BLEU

2 whole boneless chicken breasts
Salt and pepper to taste
4 slices Swiss cheese
4 slices cooked ham, 1/8 inch thick
6 tbsp. flour
2 eggs, beaten
1 tbsp. water
6 tbsp. fine dry bread crumbs
4 tbsp. butter

Remove skin from chicken breasts and discard. Between two pieces of wax paper, flatten breasts with a wooden mallet until quite thin. Cut each into 2 pieces crosswise. Season to taste with salt and pepper.

Lay a slice of cheese and slice of ham on each piece of breast and roll. Mix eggs with water and dip chicken in egg, then in flour, then in egg again and finally in crumbs. Melt butter in a flat baking dish and bake chicken at 350 degrees for 20 minutes or until lightly browned. Makes 4 servings.

NANA'S CHICKEN AND BISCUITS

1 Reynolds oven cooking bag
2 tbsp. flour
1 (15 to 16 oz.) pkg. gravy mix, chicken
1 1/2 c. water
1 can refrigerated buttermilk biscuits
6-8 chicken drumsticks (or 4 chicken breasts or 6-8 thighs)
4 med. carrots, sliced
2 stalks celery, sliced
1/4 tsp. garlic powder
Salt and pepper

Preheat oven to 350 degrees. Shake flour in Reynolds oven cooking bag. Place in 9x13 inch baking dish. Add gravy mix, garlic powder, and water. Squeeze bag to blend ingredients. Place carrots and celery in bag in even layer. Sprinkle chicken with seasonings; place on top of vegetables. Arrange biscuits around chicken.

Close bag with nylon tie; cut 6-inch slits in top. Bake until chicken is tender, 50-55 minutes. Last 10 minutes, pour 1 can drained peas into bag and continue baking; be careful not to burn yourself as steam may escape baking bag when opened. Serves 4.

CHEESY TOMATO BASIL CHICKEN BREASTS

--SAUCE--

3 tbsp. butter or margarine
2 c. cubed ripe tomatoes
1/3 c. chopped onion
6 oz. can tomato paste
1 tbsp. basil leaves
1/2 tsp. salt
1/4 tsp. pepper
2 tsp. minced fresh garlic
3 whole boneless chicken breasts,
  skinned, cut in half

--TOPPING--

1 c. fresh bread crumbs
1/2 c. chopped fresh parsley
2 tbsp. butter or margarine, melted
6 oz. Mozzarella cheese, cut into strips

Heat oven to 350 degrees. In 9x13 inch baking pan, melt 3 tablespoon butter in oven. In medium bowl, stir together remaining sauce ingredients except chicken; set aside. Place chicken in baking pan, turning to coat with butter. Spoon sauce mixture over chicken. Bake 30 to 40 minutes until chicken is no longer pink.

Meanwhile, in small bowl stir together all topping ingredients except cheese. Place cheese strips over chicken; sprinkle with topping mix. Continue baking 5 to 10 minutes or until chicken is fork tender and bread crumbs are brown.

CHICKEN BREAST SOUTHWESTERN

--MARINADE--

2/3 c. vegetable oil
1/3 c. lime juice
2 tbsp. chopped green chilies
1 tsp. minced fresh garlic
2 whole boneless, skinless chicken breasts, halved
8 slices Cheddar cheese
Salsa

In 9-inch baking pan, stir together all marinade ingredients. Add chicken breasts, marinate, turning once in refrigerator at least 45 minutes. Prepare grill.

Remove chicken from marinade. Drain. Grill chicken 7 minutes, turn. Continue grilling until fork tender. Top each piece with cheese. Continue grilling until cheese melts. Serve with salsa.

MARINATED CHICKEN

--SAUCE--

2 cans pineapple juice
1 c. cooking sherry
1/2 c. soy sauce
1/3 c. sugar

Soak skinless, boned chicken overnight. Cook about 1/2 hour over low coals; longer if done in the oven. Serve over rice.

CHICKEN TIDBITS

2 whole chicken breasts, skinned and boned
1/4 c. butter
2 tsp. Dijon style mustard
1 garlic clove, crushed or garlic salt to taste

1 tbsp. minced parsley
1 tsp. lemon juice
1/4 c. fine dry bread crumbs
1/4 c. grated Parmesan cheese

Cut chicken breasts into 3/4 inch cubes. In medium skillet, melt butter. Stir mustard, garlic, parsley, lemon juice in. Add chicken.

Saute over medium heat 5-10 minutes, turning chicken constantly. Add bread crumbs and Parmesan cheese and coat chicken evenly. Spoon into serving dish.

Serve warm or as an hors d'oeuvre or with rice as a main dish.

YOGURT CHICKEN PAPRIKA

3 tbsp. margarine
1 1/3 c. thinly sliced onion
1 tbsp. paprika
2 1/2 to 3 lb. broiler-fryer chicken, cut up
1 tsp. salt
1 c. hot water
1 chicken bouillon cube
1/4 tsp. pepper
1 tbsp. cornstarch
1 tbsp. cold water
8 oz. carton plain yogurt

Saute onion in margarine until golden; blend in paprika. Add chicken, brown well. Dissolve bouillon cube in hot water, add to skillet with salt and pepper. Cover and simmer 35-45 minutes until chicken is very tender. Dissolve cornstarch in cold water, blend into yogurt. Stir into skillet. Heat through. Serve with Spaetzles, dumplings or noodles. Serves 6.

CHICKEN PAPRIKA

5 lb. chicken pieces
3 tbsp. butter
3 tbsp. oil
1 1/2 c. finely chopped onion

3-4 tsp. sweet Hungarian paprika
4 tsp. chicken bouillon (4 cubes)
3-4 c. water (just to cover)
2 tbsp. flour mixed with 2 c. sour cream

Boil butter, oil, onion, paprika, bouillon and water in a heavy pot, add chicken. Simmer covered until tender.

Remove chicken, then bone and skin. Add flour and sour cream mixture and chicken. Don't boil again. Serve with cooked rice. Makes 6 servings.

CHICKEN AND STUFFING

1/2 chicken, cooked and broken into sm. pieces
1 pkg. Stove Top stuffing
1 can cream of chicken soup
3/4 can milk

Mix stuffing mix according to package. Place pieces of chicken in bottom of 8x8 inch pan. Top with stuffing. Mix soup with milk which will be lumpy. Pour over all. Cover with aluminum foil and bake for 25 minutes at 350 degrees.

SOFT CHICKEN TACOS

10 med. flour tortillas
1/4 c. chopped onion
2 tbsp. butter or margarine
1 (8 oz.) can tomato sauce
1/2 tsp. garlic salt
1/2 tsp. salt
1/2 tsp. ground cumin

In skillet, quickly cook 4 chicken breast fillets, cut into 1/4 inch wide strips, and onion in fat until chicken is done and onion is tender. Add tomato sauce, garlic salt, salt, and cumin. Reduce heat and simmer, covered for 15-20 minutes. To serve, place hot meat mixture on heated tortillas and top with choice of fillings. Roll up burrito style.

Makes 10 servings. FILLING CHOICES: Shredded cheese, chopped tomatoes, shredded lettuce, sliced pitted ripe olives, and taco sauce.

LOU'S LUCKY CHICKEN AND MACARONI

1 lb. chicken, cubed
1 lb. spiral macaroni
1 pkg. frozen, chopped broccoli
1 can mushroom pieces
2 sticks margarine
Garlic powder to taste

Cook and drain macaroni. Set aside. Cook broccoli according to directions. Drain and set aside. Fry chicken cubes. Add chicken, broccoli, mushrooms, and melted margarine to macaroni and season to taste with salt, pepper, and garlic powder.

CHICKEN MARSALA ALA DAN GARRIS

8 chicken breast halves or thighs
1/2 c. seasoned bread crumbs
1/4 c. Parmesan cheese
1/2 tsp. garlic powder
1 tbsp. oil
1/2 c. water
1/4 c. melted margarine or butter
1/3 c. Marsala wine or sherry

Place bread crumbs, cheese, and garlic powder in a plastic bag; add chicken pieces one at a time and shake to coat chicken. Place in shallow baking dish with oil and water. Shake remainder of bread crumb mixture over chicken. Drizzle the melted butter or margarine over the top of the chicken. Bake uncovered for 45 minutes at 350 degrees. Then add Marsala or sherry, cover with foil and continue to bake at 325 degrees for an additional 15 minutes.

CITY CHICKEN

2 lb. pork plus 2 lb. veal, cut into cubes

*Surprise--No Chicken!! Place on small wooden sticks. Beat eggs, dip meat, roll in flour, egg, then corn flake crumbs. Brown in frying pan. Place meat in roaster pan with

1 cup water and drippings from frying pan. Sprinkle with garlic. Bake uncovered at 350 degrees for 1 hour.

Great with Greek salad and flat bread. Old time favorite.

COUNTRY CHICKEN

3-6 boneless chicken breasts, cut into 2-3 inch strips
6 slices Swiss cheese
1 can cream of chicken soup
1/2 can milk
2 c. mixed stuffing
1/4 c. melted butter

Place chicken in bottom of casserole, lay cheese over top. Add soup and milk, pour over chicken.

Mix together stuffing and melted butter and pour over chicken. Bake at 325 degrees for 1 1/2 hours.

CHICKEN AND WILD RICE

1 1/2 cooked chickens, remove skin and bones
1 box Uncle Ben's wild rice
2 c. water
1/2 c. chopped green pepper
2 cans cream of mushroom soup
1 soup can milk
Salt and pepper to taste
1 (8 oz.) pkg. Pepperidge Farm stuffing mix
2 sticks butter

Fill bottom of 9x13 inch pan with cooked chicken. Cook rice in 2 cups water and mix with chicken. Add green pepper, soup, milk, salt and pepper. Mix.

Melt butter and mix with stuffing. Sprinkle on top of casserole. Bake at 350 degrees for 30-40 minutes. Cover pan with foil before baking.

LEMON-TARRAGON CHICKEN

2 tbsp. margarine
8 med. skinless, boneless chicken breast halves (1 1/2 lb.)
2 c. fresh mushrooms, halved
2 cloves garlic, minced
3 tbsp. dry sherry
1/2 tsp. tarragon, crushed
1/2 tsp. lemon pepper seasoning
1 (14 1/2 oz.) can chicken broth
1/4 c. sour cream
Hot cooked spinach or egg noodles
Quartered fresh lemon slices (optional)
1/3 c. flour

In 12-inch skillet, melt margarine over medium high heat. Add chicken, mushrooms, garlic, sherry, tarragon, and lemon pepper seasoning. Cook, uncovered, for 10-12 minutes or until chicken is no longer pink, turning once. Remove chicken and mushrooms with a slotted spoon.

In a screw top jar, combine chicken broth and flour; shake until blended. Add mixture to the skillet. Cook and stir over medium high heat until thickened and bubbly.

Remove about 1/2 cup of mixture from skillet and stir into sour cream. Return to skillet along with chicken and mushrooms. Heat through; do not boil. Serve over hot cooked noodles. Garnish with lemon slices, if desired. Serves 8.

CHICKEN IN CHEESE SAUCE

--WHITE SAUCE--

2 tbsp. butter
1/2 tsp. salt
1/8 tsp. pepper

 Mix together above over low heat in saucepan, then add: 1 c. milk
1 c. sharp Cheddar cheese
1/4 c. sherry
Dash of hot pepper

Stir over heat until sauce thickens and cheese melts. Broccoli spears

Slices of chicken breast, parboiled Place broccoli spears on bottom of baking dish with slices of chicken breasts. Pour sauce over chicken, sprinkle Parmesan or Romano cheese. Bake at 350 degrees for 30 minutes, serve over rice.

CHICKEN BREASTS

1/2 c. salad dressing
2 tbsp. Dijon mustard
1 tbsp. honey
4 boneless, skinless chicken breast halves (about 1 1/4 lb.)

Mix salad dressing, mustard and honey. Place chicken breasts on grill or rack of broiler pan; brush with half of dressing mixture. Grill or broil 8 minutes; turn brush with remaining dressing. Continue grilling or broiling 8-10 minutes longer or until tender.

CHICKEN FINGERS

5 lb. boneless chicken breasts
1 1/2 c. mayonnaise
3 tsp. minced onion
3 tsp. dry or regular mustard
2 c. dry bread crumbs
2 c. sesame seeds

Combine mayonnaise, onion, and mustard. Cut chicken into finger-sized pieces. Roll chicken in mixture. Combine bread crumbs and sesame seeds. Roll chicken in dry mixture. Place on cookie sheet, drizzle with oil and bake 15-20 minutes at 400 degrees. Serve plain or with honey dip.
 --HONEY DIP--

2 c. mayonnaise
4 tbsp. honey

 Mix together. Refrigerate until ready to serve.

CHICKEN DIVAN

1 1/2 to 2 lb. deboned, skinned chicken breasts, cut into pieces
2 tbsp. oil
1 pkg. broccoli, flowerets or cut broccoli
1 c. chicken broth
1 can cream of mushroom soup
1 2/3 c. Minute rice

cook chicken in the oil until done, approx. 5-7 minutes (can also check with a Meat Themometer) Add broth, broccoli and soup and bring mixture to a boil. Now, stir in rice, cover and remove from heat. Let sit 5 minutes. Top with Parmesan cheese, if desired. Makes 4 servings.

QUICK AND EASY CHICKEN MARINADE

1/2 c. oil
1 c. vinegar
1 1/2 tsp. poultry seasoning
2 tbsp. salt
1/4 tsp. pepper
1 egg
Paprika

Mix together all ingredients. Add 1 large or 2 small chickens. Refrigerate several hours.

CHICKEN, VEGETABLE, RICE CASSEROLE

4 chicken breasts
1/3 c. Italian dressing
2/3 c. rice, uncooked
1 (16 oz.) bag frozen broccoli, carrots, water chestnuts, etc.
1 can French fried onions
1 3/4 can c. chicken broth
1/2 tsp. Italian spices

Pour salad dressing over chicken fillets in 8x12 inch pan. Bake at 400 degrees uncovered for about 10 minutes, if frozen (if not, 5 minutes). Place rice, vegetables, and half of onions over chicken. Combine broth and seasonings.

Pour over all. Bake additional 25 minutes. Top with remaining onions. Bake 2 minutes.

BEMA'S CHICKEN AND RICE CASSEROLE

6 split chicken breasts, rolled in poultry seasons and parsley
1/2 lb. margarine
1 c. chopped green pepper
1 c. chopped onion
4 c. chicken broth (2 cans sweet sue)
1 c. rice (Uncle Ben's wild and long rice works well)

Place chicken breasts skin side down into baking dish with margarine and bake at 350 degrees for 30 min.

Remove breasts temporarily, stir in peppers and onions, add rice. Place chicken on top skin side up. Bake at 350 degrees for at least an hour. This is a nice make ahead dish suitable not only for family but for company as well.

CHICKEN CACCIATORE

4 whole chicken breasts (8 halves)
3 (7 oz.) cans tomato paste
8 cans water
2 peppers
2 onions
1 clove garlic, crushed
1 (8 oz.) can mushrooms, stems and pieces
Oil
Basil
parsley
Salt and pepper
6 oz. wine

Put oil in bottom of pan to cover. Brown garlic and slice 2 onions very thin and brown. Add mushrooms. Add 3 cans tomato paste and cook on low for 15 minutes. Add 8 cans water, salt, pepper, basil, and parsley. Cook for 3/4 hour. Fry sliced peppers until soft and set aside. Brown chicken (coat first with flour, salt, and pepper), then fry in hot oil. Put chicken, peppers, sauce, and mushrooms in a large pan and mix well. If it "hugs" chicken too much, add 1 can water. Cook about another hour, or so, or until chicken is soft. Add wine last 20 minutes.

CHICKEN PICCATA

4 chicken breasts
1 egg
6 tbsp. lemon
2 chicken bouillon cubes
1/2 c. flour
Shake of garlic powder and paprika
4 tbsp. butter

Mix egg with 1 tablespoon lemon. Mix flour with garlic powder and paprika. Dip chicken in egg, then flour mixture.

Place immediately in frying pan with butter melted. Brown. While it is cooking, dissolve boiling water with bouillon cube and lemon juice. After chicken is browned, pour bouillon mixture over chicken; simmer gently covered for 20 minutes. Liquid mixture can be doubled for more gravy.

ORIENTAL CHICKEN WONTONS

8 oz. ground raw chicken
1/2 c. shredded carrots
1/4 c. finely chopped celery or water chestnuts
1 tbsp. soy sauce
1 tbsp. dry sherry
2 tsp. cornstarch
2 tsp. grated gingerroot
1/2 (16 oz.) pkg. wonton wrappers
2 tbsp. margarine or butter, melted
Plum or Sweet & Sour Sauce

Filling: In a medium skillet cook and stir ground chicken until no pink remains; drain. Stir in carrots, celery or waterchestnuts, soy sauce, sherry, cornstarch and gingerroot; mix well. Spoon 1 rounded teaspoon of the filling atop a wonton wrapper, lightly brush edges with water. To shape each wonton, carefully bring 2 opposite points of the square wrapper up over the filling and pinch together in the center. Carefully bring the 2 remaining opposite points to the center and pinch together. Pinch together edges to seal. Place wontons on a greased baking sheet. Brush the wontons with melted margarine or butter. Bake in a 375 degree oven for 8-10 minutes or until lightly brown and crisp. Serve with Plum or Sweet & Sour Sauce. Makes about 25 appetizer servings.

CURRY CHICKEN

1 pkg. chicken wing drumettes (3-4 lb.) or
1 med. sized chicken (3-4 lb.), cut into sm. pieces
3 tsp. curry powder
1 tsp. salt
1/4 tsp. black pepper
1/4 tsp. crushed red pepper
2 tsp. sugar
1 1/2 c. water
1/2 of an onion, diced

Optional: 1 teaspoon of lemon grass powder or fresh lemon grass chop into fine pieces. Lemon grass can only be purchased at an oriental food store. Put water in a pan big enough to hold all ingredients. Add all spices. Stir until mixed. Add chicken and onion. Cook on high until boiling, then lower temperature to medium. Stir well, then cover. Cook (covered) until sauce has thickened and chicken is well-cooked (approximately 30-40 minutes). Stir every 10 minutes so chicken is coated evenly with the sauce. More water can be added if a thinner sauce is desired. Serve with steamed rice. 4-6 servings.

CHICKEN WITH RICE

1 med. onion, chopped
2 tbsp. butter
1 tbsp. olive oil
2 lb. chicken breasts, thighs or drumsticks
Salt & pepper
3 tbsp. dry, white wine
1 lb. fresh tomatoes, peeled & chopped
1/2 c. tomato sauce
1 c. rice
1/4 c. butter
Grated Romano or Parmesan cheese

In a large saucepan, saute onion in butter and oil. Add chicken to onion and brown well on all sides; salt and pepper lightly. Add wine and simmer 5 minutes. Stir in tomatoes and tomato sauce diluted in 2 cups of water; simmer 15 minutes or until chicken is tender. Remove chicken to platter; cover and set aside. Measure liquid; add hot water to equal 3 cups. Bring to a boil; add rice and simmer 20 minutes or until rice is tender. Stir occasionally. Adjust seasoning if needed. Gently melt butter and pour over rice. Top with chicken; cover and keep warm. To serve, spoon rice on platter, surround with chicken and sprinkle generously with cheese

----

FAJITA - STYLE CHICKEN BREASTS

--MARINADE--

2/3 c. vegetable oil
1/3 c. lime juice
2 tbsp. chopped green chilies
2 cloves garlic, chopped

Prepare grill. In a 9 inch square baking pan, stir together all marinade ingredients. Add 2 whole chicken breasts, skinned and halved. Marinade for at least 45 minutes in the refrigerator. Turn once. Remove chicken from marinade and drain. Grill chicken over hot coals 7 minutes. Continue grilling until fork tender (6-8 minutes). Top each piece of chicken with 2 slices Cheddar cheese and grill until cheese begins to melt. Serve with salsa.

TERIYAKI CHICKEN

1 c. soy sauce
1 c. sugar
3 cloves garlic
Ginger slice
3-4 split chickens

Bake at 350 degrees for 1 hour. Baste while cooking and bake in all the sauce

CHICKEN AND PORK ADOBO

1/2 lb. chicken breast
1/2 lb. lean pork
1 c. soy sauce
1/4 c. vinegar
2 tbsp. sugar
1/4 tsp. pepper
4 cloves garlic

Cut chicken and pork in small pieces. Mix with sauce. Cook for 1/2 hour or until tender. Serve hot.

APPLE CHICKEN CASSEROLE

3 unpeeled tart apples, cubed
2 chicken breasts, skinned
2 tbsp. orange juice
2 tbsp. honey
2 orange slices

Place apples in bottom of lightly oiled casserole dish. Put chicken breasts over apples. Combine orange juice and honey in a cup. Spoon 1 tablespoon of mixture over each piece. Cover casserole and bake 45 minutes at 350 degrees. Uncover casserole. Spoon remaining orange juice and honey over chicken and bake another 30 minutes, uncovered. Garnish with orange slices.

SAUTEED CHICKEN LIVERS

1 lb. chicken livers
Butter
Paprika
Salt & pepper
Flour

In a plastic bag; put flour, salt, pepper, paprika and season all (or) poultry seasoning. Add the chicken livers and shake them all about, until coated. Put them into frying pan with butter added and fry until well done and brown.

POTTED CHICKEN

3 lb. chicken parts
6 c. bubbling water
2 onions, peeled & quartered
3 carrots, thickly sliced
2 1/2 tsp. seasoned salt
1 (10 oz.) pkg. frozen mixed vegetables
1 pkg. chicken noodle soup mix
4 tsp. parsley
1 bay leaf, crumbled

Boil first 5 ingredients and cook 20 minutes or until chicken is tender. Add the remaining ingredients and cook done but not mushy.

CHICKEN RICE BAKE

1 1/2 c. regular rice
1 can cream of mushroom soup
1 can cream of chicken soup
1 can cream of celery soup
1 3/4 c. milk
1 cut up fryer
1 pkg. onion soup mix

Grease bottom of 13 x 9 x 2 inch pan. Add rice to make bottom layer. Combine soups and milk. Heat and pour over rice. Lay chicken pieces on top. Scatter onion soup mix over top. Cover with foil. Bake in slow oven (325 degrees) for 2 hours.

TOM'S CHICKEN ENCHILADAS

12 corn tortillas
Salad oil
Cream Cheese Filling (below)
2/3 c. whipping cream
2 c. shredded Jack cheese
2 lg. onions
2 tbsp. butter
2 c. diced cooked chicken or turkey
1/2 c. sweet red peppers or pimento
2 sm. (3 oz.) pkg. cream cheese

Fry tortillas. Drain on paper towels. Cook onions in butter until limp. Combine onions, chicken, pimento and cream cheese. Mix lightly, salt to taste. Spoon 1/3 cup filling into tortillas, roll and place seam side down in 9 x 13 inch baking dish side by side. Moisten tops of tortillas with whipping cream. Sprinkle with cheese. Bake uncovered in 375 degree oven 20 minutes to heat through. May serve with lime wedges to squeeze on each serving. Very mild flavor.

CHICKEN FRIED STEAK

2 lb. beef round steak
1 egg, beaten
1 tbsp. milk
1 c. crushed saltine crackers
Salt & pepper to taste
Cooking oil for frying

Pound the steak with knife, cut into serving pieces. Blend egg and milk. Mix on separate plate, cracker crumbs, salt and pepper. Dip meat into egg mixture then crackers. Brown meat on both sides in hot oil, then turn heat down to simmer, cover skillet and cook until tender 40-45 minutes. Gravy for meat: Remove meat when done from pan, add a little water/flour mixture to drippings. Bring to a boil. Then simmer until desired consistency.

ITALIAN CHICKEN

1 frying chicken, cut up
2 tbsp. melted butter
Salt & pepper
2 tbsp. dry Italian salad dressing mix
1 can condensed mushroom soup
2 (3 oz.) pkg. cream cheese (cut into cubes)

Wash chicken and pat dry. Brush with butter. Sprinkle with salt and pepper. Place in slow cooker. Sprinkle dry salad mix over. Cover and cook on low for 5-6 hours. About 3/4 hours before serving, mix soup and cream cheese.

Cook until smooth. Pour over chicken in pot. Cover and cook 30 minutes on low.

SO EASY OVEN - FRIED CHICKEN

1 frying chicken, cut into 8 pieces
1/4 lb. melted butter
1/8 tsp. garlic powder
1/8 tsp. paprika
1/8 tsp. thyme
1 tsp. salt
1 1/2 c. dry bread crumbs, finely crushed cornflakes or flour

Dip chicken pieces in butter, then shake in paper bag containing remaining dry ingredients. Place skin side up in lightly greased 9 x 13 inch baking dish and bake 50 minutes at 350 degrees or until done. Serves 6-8.

MEXICAN CHICKEN CASSEROLE

6 chicken breast or 1 whole chicken
1 can cream of mushroom soup
10 oz. Velveeta cheese
1 can Rotel tomatoes
1 c. milk
1 bag Doritos

Boil chicken. Debone and chop up chicken. Combine milk, Velveeta, soup and tomatoes; bring to a boil. Add meat and simmer 5-10 minutes, stirring often. Put layer of Doritos in long casserole dish, then layer meat mixture.

Add layer of chips, layer of meat mixture, ending with chips on top. Bake at 350 degrees for 30 minutes.

CHICKEN POT PIE

2 pie shells
2 cans mixed vegetables
Whole chicken
1 stick butter

Take chicken and boil until done. Put 1 pie shell on bottom of deep deep dish. Take chicken off the bones. Then mix chicken, chicken broth with mixed vegetables and butter. Then pour over pie shell. Then put the other pie shell on top. Bake for 45 minutes at 325 degrees.

CHICKEN POT PIE

4 chicken breasts
1 can cream of chicken soup
1 c. chicken broth
1 c. milk
1 bag frozen peas & carrots
5-6 boiled eggs
Salt & pepper to taste
1 stick of butter
1 can flaky biscuits (10 ct.)

Boil chicken until done. Cook peas and carrots. Mix 1 can cream of chicken soup, broth, milk, melted butter, salt and pepper. Simmer until sauce thickens. Then layer chicken, sauce, vegetables, boiled eggs, sauce and biscuits. Tear biscuits apart and completely cover. Bake to directions or biscuits until biscuits are brown.

EASY CHICKEN POT PIE

2 cans (10 3/4 oz. each) cream of potato soup
1 (16 oz.) can Veg-All
2 c. cooked, diced chicken
1/2 c. milk
1/2 tsp. thyme
1/2 tsp. black pepper
2 (9") frozen pie crust, thawed

Combine first 6 ingredients. Spoon into 1 pie crust. Cover with other pie crust; crimp edges to seal. Slit top crust. Bake at 375 degrees for 40 minutes. Cool 10 minutes.

SOUR CREAM AND CHICKEN ENCHILADAS

6 boneless chicken breast
8 flour tortillas
8 oz. sour cream
1 jar picante sauce
2 c. Monterey Jack cheese

Boil chicken breast. Cut into slices. Simmer chicken in picante sauce. Lightly spread butter on flour tortillas.

Stuff tortillas with chicken mixture. Lay open side face down in casserole dish. Cut slices in top of tortillas.

Spread sour cream then cheese on top of tortillas. Bake at 350 degrees about 30 minutes until cheese is melted.

THYME CHICKEN

4 boneless chicken breasts
1/2 pt. whipping cream
1 stick butter
Thyme
Salt & pepper to taste
Sliced fresh mushrooms

Melt stick of butter in skillet. Wash and dry chicken. Fry chicken in butter until golden brown. Take chicken out

and sprinkle with thyme. Saute mushrooms in butter. Return chicken to skillet with mushrooms and pour cream over these. Cook until cream thickens and turns brown. This is delicious served with a rice casserole and green bean casserole.

CHICKEN CASSEROLE

1 can Rotel tomatoes with chilies
1 can cream of mushroom soup
1 sm. Velveeta cheese, diced
1 sm. onion, sauteed
1 stick margarine
1 whole chicken
1 c. Cheddar cheese
1 pack spaghetti

Boil chicken and take off bone. In the same water, boil spaghetti and drain, but do not rinse. Mix all ingredients together, except Cheddar cheese. Bake at 350 degrees until Velveeta cheese is melted and hot. Garnish with Cheddar cheese and serve.

CHICKEN SPAGHETTI

5 chicken breasts
1 can cream of chicken soup
1 (8 oz.) pkg. Velveeta, grated
1 (8 oz.) pkg. spaghetti noodles

Boil chicken with skin intact, approximately 25 minutes, with salt and pepper. Remove boiled chicken, remove skin and bone. Boil spaghetti in broth. Spray 9 x 13 inch pan with Pam. Place chicken pieces, soup, cheese, 1 1/2 cups of chicken broth and cooked spaghetti in pan and bake at 350 degrees for 35 minutes.

CHICKEN SPAGHETTI

1 whole chicken, cooked & boned
1 can Rotel tomatoes
1 lb. Velveeta cheese
Spaghetti
1 onion
1 bell pepper

Saute onion and bell pepper in butter. Add cheese (cubed) and let it melt. Add can of Rotel. Cook spaghetti, drain and mix all ingredients.

MOZZARELLA CHICKEN AND SAUCE

4 chicken breast with or without bones
1 jar Ragu spaghetti sauce (tomatoes and herbs)
1/2 green bell pepper, chopped
1 sm. onion, chopped
1/4 c. sliced ham, chopped
1 c. mozzarella cheese
Dales steak sauce
Salt, pepper & garlic powder to taste

Cover bottom of Pyrex dish (for oven) with Dales steak sauce. Layer bottom of dish with chicken (browning optional). Sprinkle chicken with onions, green peppers, salt, pepper, garlic powder and ham. Cover with Ragu sauce. Cover and cook for 50 minutes in preheated oven, 350 degree cooking temperature. Remove cover and cover with cheese. Remain cooking until cheese melts, about 5 minutes. Serve over spaghetti noodles and with French bread. Yield 4 servings as a complete meal.

CHICKEN WITH MOZZARELLA CHEESE

6 chicken breasts
3 eggs, beaten & salted
Progresso bread crumbs
2 tbsp. melted butter
4 tbsp. cooking oil
1 (10 1/2 oz.) can cream of chicken soup

1 c. chicken broth
8 oz. mozzarella cheese slices

Dip chicken pieces in beaten eggs, roll in bread crumbs and brown in oil and butter. Place in casserole dish.

Combine soup and broth. Pour over chicken and bake covered at 350 degrees for 30 minutes. Place slices of cheese over chicken and bake 10 more minutes uncovered. Serve with rice.

SWISS CHEESE CHICKEN CASSEROLE

4-6 chicken breasts
6 slices Swiss cheese
1 can cream of mushroom soup
1/4 c. milk
2 c. Pepperidge Farm herb seasoning stuffing mix
1/4 c. margarine

Place chicken in casserole lightly greased. Place cheese on top of chicken. Mix soup and milk; pour over chicken.

Cover mixture up stuffing mix. Drizzle butter over crumbs. Cover and bake at 350 degrees for 50 minutes.

CHICKEN DIVAN

1 can cream of chicken soup
1 (8 oz.) pkg. sour cream
8 oz. shredded Cheddar cheese
4-6 chicken breasts
3/4 c. chicken broth
Bread crumbs
Butter or margarine
1 bunch fresh broccoli or lg. pkg. frozen

Preheat oven to 375 degrees. Boil and debone chicken. Reserve 3/4 cup broth. Place uncooked broccoli in bottom of 8 1/2 x 11 inch casserole dish. Top with chicken pieces. In small mixing bowl, stir together soup, sour cream and chicken broth. Pour over chicken. Top with cheese. Sprinkle with bread crumbs and dot with butter. Bake about 1 minute until cheese is golden brown.

CHICKEN AND BROCCOLI CASSEROLE

4 chicken breast fillets
1 lb. broccoli, frozen
1 can cream of mushroom soup
1 can cream of chicken soup
1 (8 oz.) Velveeta cheese
1/2 box Ritz crackers

Cut chicken fillets into bite-size pieces. Saute in butter until it turns white. Cook broccoli according to directions on package. Mix chicken and broccoli. Place in an 8 x 8 inch casserole dish. Melt Velveeta cheese in microwave.

Add both cans of soup to cheese. Pour over chicken and broccoli. Stir until well mixed. Top with crushed Ritz crackers. Bake at 350 degrees for approximately 30 minutes until brown.

CHICKEN LALA PIE

1 pkg. family size chicken
1 (8 oz.) sour cream
1 pkg. Stove Top stuffing
1/2 stick butter
1 (8 oz.) can cream of mushroom soup

Preparation time: 400 degrees. Cooking time: 45 minutes. Boil chicken, let cool and debone. Chop chicken into bite-size. Lay in bottom of casserole pan.

Mix sour cream and cream of mushroom soup together and spread over chicken. Use 3 cups of broth (leftover from boiling chicken), 1/2 stick of butter, let butter melt. Mix season mix from box of stuffing into broth. Then blend stuffing.

Spread over top of casserole. Bake at 400 degrees for 45 minutes.

CHICKEN TETRAZZINI

1 chicken
8 oz. vermicelli
1/2 c. chopped bell pepper
1 lg. chopped onion
2 cans mushroom soup
1/4 tsp. celery salt
1/2 tsp. black pepper
1 tbsp. Worcestershire sauce
3/4 lb. Cheddar cheese, grated

Remove chicken from bone and cut in bite-size pieces. Cook bell pepper and onion in 1 cup chicken broth. Cook vermicelli in remainder of broth real slow. Mix all ingredients. Heat 25 minutes at 350 degrees.

CHICKEN AND BISCUITS

3 tbsp. margarine
3 chicken breasts, cooked & boned
3 tbsp. chopped onion
3 tbsp. chopped celery
2 tbsp. Worcestershire sauce
2/3 drops Tabasco
Salt & pepper to taste
1 can (10 count) Hungry Jack buttermilk biscuits & 1 sm. can
1 can cream of mushroom or chicken soup
1/2 c. sour cream
1/2 c. milk
2 c. grated Cheddar cheese

Cut chicken up into very small pieces. In a skillet melt margarine and saute onion and celery. Add Worcestershire sauce, Tabasco, salt and pepper. Add cut up chicken to this mixture. In a bowl, mix soup, sour cream and milk; set aside. With a rolling pin, roll each biscuit out flat. Put a spoonful of chicken mixture on each biscuit, fold biscuit over and pinch all edges together. Place biscuits in lightly greased baking dish and bake 10-15 minutes at 400 degrees or until lightly brown. Remove from oven and cover with soup mixture and grated cheese and return to oven for 10-15 minutes until cheese and soup are bubbly.

CHEESE `N CHICKEN ENCHILADAS

1 med. onion, chopped
2 tbsp. margarine
1 1/2 c. shredded cooked chicken
1 jar picante sauce
8 flour tortillas (6")
1 pkg. (3 oz.) cream cheese, cubed
1 tsp. ground cumin
2 c. shredded extra sharp Cheddar cheese

Heat oven to 350 degrees. Cook and stir onion in large skillet until tender. Stir in chicken, 1/4 cup of picante sauce, cream cheese and cumin; cook until thoroughly heated. Stir in 1 cup of cheese. Spoon about 1/3 cup chicken mixture in center of each tortilla; roll up. Place seam side down in 12 x 7 inch baking dish. Top with remaining picante sauce and cheese. Bake 15 minutes.

CHICKEN & RICE CASSEROLE

1 c. uncooked rice
1 can cream of chicken soup
1 pkg. Good Season Italian dressing mix
2 c. boiling water
2 1/2-3 lb. cut up chicken or chicken breasts

Wash and drain rice. Spread in 9 x 13 inch baking dish or 3 quart casserole. Mix soup, Italian dressing mix and water. Stir into rice, salt and pepper, chicken pieces. Lay skin side up on top of rice mixture. Cover tightly with foil and cook for 1 hour at 350 degrees. Uncover and cook for 20 minutes longer to dry rice.

Put casserole under broiler for a few seconds to brown chicken. Serves 6-8. *Cream of mushroom soup can be substituted for the cream of chicken soup.

SWEET & SOUR CHICKEN

2 pkg. boneless chicken
2 bell peppers
1 lg. onion
1 tbsp. flour
2 jars Sweet & Sour Sauce

1 c. flour
1 c. oil
Salt & pepper as desired

Heat 1 cup oil. Wash chicken pieces and dry, salt and pepper as desired. Roll chicken in cup of flour and deep fry until crispy. Remove and drain. Drain all but a small amount of oil from skillet and saute onion and bell pepper for 5 minutes.

Add chicken and 1 tablespoon of flour to onions and peppers; saute for 5 additional minutes. Add sweet and sour sauce to contents. Cover and allow to simmer for 15 minutes. Serve over rice.

CHICKEN BREAST CASSEROLE

8 chicken breast
1 can cream of chicken soup
1 tbsp. grated onion
1 tbsp. lemon juice
3 tbsp. mayonnaise
1/2 c. slivered almonds (optional)

Cook chicken breast, until tender. Remove skin and bones and cut chicken breast in half. Mix sauce and arrange breast in a Pyrex dish. Allow room between breasts. Put sauce on each breast separately. Just before baking put crushed potato chips or Ritz crackers, or corn flakes on top. Bake at 400 degrees for 20 minutes.

CHICKEN AND BROCCOLI CASSEROLE

2 c. cooked, chopped chicken
2 (10 oz.) pkgs. frozen broccoli
2 cans cream of chicken soup
3/4 c. mayonnaise
1/2 tsp. lemon juice
1/2 tsp. curry powder
1/2 c. grated cheese or more
1/2 c. Pepperidge Farm stuffing mix or more

Cook broccoli until just tender in salted water. Put in large baking dish. Place cooked, chopped chicken over broccoli. Combine soup, lemon juice, curry and mayonnaise. Mix well. Spread over chicken. Top with cheese.

Sprinkle with stuffing mix. Bake at 350 degrees for 25 to 30 minutes.

HOT CHICKEN SALAD

4 c. diced chicken (6 breasts, baked)
2 c. diced celery
1/3 c. mayonnaise
1 can cream of mushroom soup
1 sm. jar chopped pimiento
1 can sliced water chestnuts, drained
1 tsp. salt
1 tsp. chopped onion
3 tsp. lemon juice
1 c. grated cheese
1 c. crushed potato chips
1/2 c. slivered almonds

Blend the first nine ingredients and pour into a 9"x13" pan. Top with the grated cheese, potato chips and slivered almonds. Bake at 350 degrees for 30 minutes. Will be bubbly.

CHEDDAR CHICKEN

1 (10 oz.) frozen chopped broccoli
2 whole chicken breasts
4 tbsp. butter
1/2 lb. shredded mild cheddar cheese
1/3 c. milk
2 tbsp. sliced almonds

Place chopped broccoli in 8"x12" baking dish. Set aside to thaw. Cut chicken in cubes, brown in butter about 10 minutes until they are fork tender. Place on broccoli. In 1 quart saucepan over low stir cheese and milk until smooth. Pour cheese mixture over chicken and broccoli. Sprinkle with almonds. Bake 20 to 30 minutes at 350 degrees, until heated through.

300 Chicken Recipes

CHICKEN CASSEROLE

1/3 c. margarine
1/3 c. flour
1 c. broth
1 c. milk
Salt & pepper to taste
1 tbsp. chopped onion
3 c. cut up chicken
1 can whole kernel corn
3/4 c. grated sharp cheese
1/4 c. pimiento

Make white sauce (first 6 ingredients). Mix all ingredients together and put in casserole dish. Put buttered bread crumbs on top and bake at 350 degrees until bubbly.

BUSY DAY CHICKEN & RICE

1 c. uncooked rice
1 chicken, cut up
1 stick oleo
1 pkg. dry onion soup mix
4 c. boiling water
Salt & pepper to taste

preheat oven to 350 degrees. Grease bottom of 13"x9"x2" pan. Cover bottom evenly with rice. Arrange chicken pieces on rice. Dot with oleo or margarine. Sprinkle dry onion soup over all. Salt and pepper to taste. Pour boiling water over all.

Bake 1 hour. If browner chicken is desired brown before placing on rice.

FESTIVE CHICKEN

2 c. chicken, cooked, chopped
1 box wild rice, cooked
1 med. onion, chopped
1/2 c. mayonnaise
1 can French green beans or 1 pkg. broccoli, cooked
1 can celery soup
1/2 c. water chestnuts (optional)
2 tbsp. chopped pimiento (optional)

Put all together into greased baking dish. Bake 45 minutes to 1 hour at 350 degrees.

CHICKEN CASSEROLE

Cook boneless/skinless chicken in salted water and chop into bite size pieces. Place in baking dish. Spread a package of dry Stove Top stuffing over chicken. Combine 1 1/2 to 2 cups chicken broth with 1 can celery soup, packet from Stove Top stuffing (vegetable/seasoning). Pour over chicken and stuffing. Bake at 350 degrees for 30 minutes.

PARMESAN CHICKEN

1 c. crushed Ritz crackers
3/4 c. Parmesan cheese
4 boneless chicken breasts
1/4 c. melted margarine

Mix 3/4 cup Parmesan cheese to each 1 cup of crushed Ritz cracker crumbs. Dip boneless chicken breasts in melted margarine and then roll in crumb mixture. Then roll chicken breast wide end to narrow end. Lay in baking dish seam side down. Bake at 350 degrees for 1 hour. Cover the first 1/2 hour of cooking and then take cover off last 1/2 hour. Increase recipe according to needs.

CHICKEN POT PIE

2 c. chicken (1 fryer or 4 breasts)
1 (20 oz.) pkg. frozen mixed vegetables
2 cans cream of chicken soup
1 c. chicken broth

--TOPPING--

1 c. self rising flour
1 stick margarine
1 c. milk

Cut chicken into chunks. May be pre-cooked. For convenience canned chicken breast may be used. Layer vegetables, chicken and soup mixture in a 2 quart greased casserole dish. Pour topping over the mixture and bake at 400 degrees for 1 hour or until golden brown.

CHICKEN CASSEROLE

1 fryer or chicken breast (stewed)
2 cans cream of chicken soup
1 pkg. Pepperidge Farm dressing mix
1 c. chicken broth
1 c. milk

Remove skin and bone from stewed chicken. Place in bottom of 13"x9" baking dish. Cover with chicken soup. Prepare dressing as directed on package. Place over chicken in dish, pour broth and milk over the top. Bake 400 degrees about 25 minutes.

CHICKEN BENGALI

1 tbsp. margarine
1 1/2 tsp. flour
1 1/2 tsp. Worcestershire sauce
1 tsp. powder mustard
1/2 tsp. curry powder
1 1/2 lbs. chicken thighs, skinned

Preheat oven to 375 degrees. In small saucepan heat margarine over medium heat until bubbly and hot. Add remaining ingredients except chicken until mixture is smooth. Put in 9"x9" baking dish sprayed with Pam. Arrange chicken in single layers. Bake until chicken is brown, baste with juice every 20 minutes. Weight Watchers.

CHICKEN SPECTACULAR

3 c. cooked chicken
1 pkg. Uncle Ben's Wild White Rice, cooked
1 can cream of celery soup
1 med. onion, chopped
2 c. French style green beans, drained
1 c. Hellmann's mayonnaise
1 c. water chestnuts, diced
1 med. jar sliced pimientos (for color, if desired)

Mix all ingredients. Pour into 2 1/2 or 3 quart casserole. Bake at 350 degrees for 25 to 30 minutes. (To freeze, do not cook before freezing.)

GOURMET CHICKEN

1 c. uncooked rice
1 can mushroom soup
1 can onion soup
1 can water
1 frying size chicken or breasts (can cut boned breasts into sm. pieces)
Salt & pepper to taste

Place uncooked rice in bottom of 9"x12" pan. Pour soups and water over rice. Mix slightly. Place chicken on top. Cut chicken (smaller pieces) can be stirred into mix.

Bake at 325 degrees 1 hour and 15 minutes.

 When using big chicken pieces, turn when browned on one side.

CHICKEN WITH PORT

Serve with an elegant dry red wine, such as Cabernet Sauvignon Sequoia Grove Vineyards 1986. Napa Valley.

2 tbsp. vegetable oil
2 tbsp. butter, room temperature
1 c. thinly sliced onions
6 lg. boneless chicken breast halves
Salt, freshly ground pepper to taste
4 cloves garlic, minced
1 c. tawny port (such as Fonseca Bin #27)
1/2 c. heavy cream
1/4 c. chopped parsley, to garnish

In a large skillet heat oil and butter over medium heat. Add onions and cook, stirring frequently, until golden brown, about 5 minutes. Add chicken and cook 4 minutes on each side, or until golden brown on outside and cooked through on inside. Season with salt and pepper.

Remove chicken with a slotted spatula to a platter; cover to keep warm. Add garlic to skillet and cook over low heat 2 minutes until garlic just releases its fragrance. Add port and boil 1 minute, or until reduced to 1/2 cup. Add chicken and boil 30 seconds, or until lightly thickened. To serve chicken, cut each breast on the diagonal into 1 inch slices. Serve with sauce; garnish with parsley.

CHICKEN IN WINE SAUCE

1 pkg. boneless chicken breasts
1 pkg. Stove Top stuffing
2 cans cream of chicken soup
1/2 c. white wine
1/4 c. water

Cook chicken breasts until done. While chicken is cooking, prepare the stuffing according to package directions. When chicken is done, cut into bite-sized pieces and place in casserole dish. Add cream of chicken soup, wine and water. Mix. Spread the prepared stuffing on top. Bake in oven at 350 degrees for 30 minutes. Freezes well.

and can be prepared ahead without baking. Bake after freezing and prior to serving. Serves 6.

CHICKEN IN WINE

6 chicken breast halves, skinless
1 can whole white onions
1 can cream of mushroom soup
1/4 c. sherry
1/4 lb. Cheddar cheese, grated

Place chicken in baking dish. Mix soup and sherry. Pour over chicken. Grate cheese over top. Bake covered for 45 minutes and uncover for 45 minutes at 350 degrees.

CHICKEN ORIENTAL

1 c. cream of mushroom soup
1 c. (8 oz.) pineapple chunks in pure pineapple juice, undrained
1 tbsp. soy sauce
2 c. Swanson chunk white chicken
1 c. each sliced celery, green onions & green pepper
1/2 c. sliced radishes
1 c. sliced water chestnuts

In a skillet, combine soup, pineapple, soy sauce and add remaining ingredients. Simmer 10 minutes. Stir gently occasionally. Serve with cooked rice and additional soy sauce. Makes about 5 1/2 cups.

EASY CHICKEN DISH

Chicken breasts, skinned One layer in oblong dish. Mix together 1 can cream of mushroom soup and 1 package Lipton onion soup. Add 1/2 cup of heavy cream. Mix and spread over chicken. Sprinkle with paprika. Bake at 350 degrees for 40 minutes.

CHICKEN CUTLETS

Chicken, cutlets or pieces, whatever
Swiss or muenster cheese
1 can cream of chicken soup
1/2 can water
1 pkg. stuffing mix
Butter or margarine

Place chicken cutlets or portions of chicken breasts in pan. Place layer of Swiss or muenster cheese on top. Add 1 can of cream of chicken soup, diluted with 1/2 can of water. Pour over the chicken and cheese. Put dry stuffing mix on top (followed by seasoning mix, if separated package). Dot with butter or margarine. Bake 45 minutes at 325 degrees.

SAUSAGE - CHICKEN DISH

1 lb. sausage
1 lb. chicken breasts
1 lg. can crushed tomatoes
1 pkg. dry onion soup mix
1 pkg. frozen spinach or broccoli (defrosted)
2 chicken bouillon cubes
Salt, pepper & garlic powder to taste

Brown sausage. Cut into 1 inch pieces. Add chicken and brown. Drain fat and add the remaining ingredients. Simmer until done. Serve with noodles.

CHICKEN ROLL UPS

4 boneless & skinless chicken breasts, pounded thin
Cream cheese
Garlic powder
Parsley
Chives
8 slices bacon

Spread a layer of cream cheese on the inside of the chicken breast. Season to taste with garlic, parsley and chives. Roll up, starting with the smallest end. Wrap 2 slices of bacon around the rolled chicken breast. Bake 30-40 minutes in a 325 degree oven or until done. Broil last 5 minutes to brown bacon.

CHICKEN ALA BELGIQUE

Marinate in 1 cup white wine: 1/2 lb. thinly sliced ham, cut julienne
3-4 diced shallots Saute in 6 tablespoons butter for 10 minutes: 8 chicken cutlets, salted, peppered & floured.

Drain ham mixture, reserving liquid. Add ham mixture to chicken and cook 5-8 minutes. Pour reserved wine mixture into chicken and ham mixture. Cook 5-8 minutes. Remove chicken to serving platter. Add to pan: 1 tbsp. Dijon mustard 1 c. heavy cream. Stir until heated through and slightly thickened. Pour over meat. Serve with rice.

EASY BARBECUE CHICKEN

1 pkg. dry onion soup mix
1 sm. bottle Russian dressing (the pink kind)
1 (8-10 oz.) jar apricot preserves

Pour over skinned chicken pieces. Bake at 350 degrees for 1 1/2 hours.

OVEN BAKED BARBECUE CHICKEN

In a saucepan melt 2 tablespoons butter. Add 2 cloves of garlic, crushed. Cook 4-5 minutes. Then add ingredients listed below.

1 c. catsup
2/3 c. chili sauce
4 tbsp. brown sugar
4 tbsp. chopped onion
2 tbsp. Worcestershire sauce
2 tbsp. prepared mustard
2 tsp. celery seed
1/2 tsp. salt
Dash of Tabasco (optional)

6 thin slices of lemon

Bring to a boil. Place chicken in a shallow pan. Pour boiling sauce over it. Bake at 350 degrees for 1 hour, basting often with sauce. Alternative method: Cover chicken and sauce and bake at 200 degrees for 2 hours, uncover and bake at 450 degrees for 20 minutes.

GINGER PEACHY CHICKEN

2 lg. chicken breasts, split
1 (18 oz.) can peach halves
2 tsp. honey
2 tbsp. peach juice
1/2 tsp. garlic salt
1/2 tsp. ground ginger

Put chicken in baking dish and arrange peach halves in between. Drizzle peach juice and honey over the top.

Sprinkle with garlic salt and ginger. Bake at 325 degrees until done. Serves 3-4 persons.

PECAN CHICKEN WITH DIJON MUSTARD

Chicken cutlets
Dijon mustard
Pecans crushed
Bread crumbs
Butter
Light cream
2 chicken bouillon cubes

Whip butter and Dijon mustard (3 to 1 Dijon to butter). Combine pecans and bread crumbs (50-50). Dip chicken in Dijon and butter mixture. Then coat with pecan/crumb mixture (pat down well). Bake at 325 degrees for 30 minutes in buttered dish.

--CREAM SAUCE--

1/8 c. flour

2 tbsp. butter
1 c. light cream
2 bouillon cubes
1 tsp. Dijon mustard

Melt butter. Add flour, then cream. Stir constantly over medium heat until sauce thickens. Add bouillon cubes. Stir until melted. Add 1 teaspoon Dijon mustard. (If sauce should get too thick, add more cream and Dijon to taste.)

CHICKEN OF PUERTO RICO

1-3 lb. chicken pieces
1 tbsp. salt
1 bay leaf
1 c. olive oil
4 tbsp. butter
1/2 lb. sliced onions
1/2 c. vinegar

Rub chicken with salt and pepper. Brown in olive oil. Arrange onions over chicken. Add butter, bay leaf and vinegar. Cover and cook until done over low heat.

CHICKEN PARMESAN

4 half chicken breasts (skinned & boned)
2 cans (14 1/2 oz. each) DelMonte Italian style stewed tomatoes
2 tbsp. cornstarch
1/2 tsp. oregano or basil crushed (I use basil)
1/4 tsp. hot pepper sauce (Tabasco sauce)
1/4 c. grated Parmesan cheese

Place chicken in baking dish. Bake covered 15 minutes in preheated 425 degree oven. Drain. Combine tomatoes, cornstarch, basil and pepper sauce. Cook stirring constantly until thickened. Pour heated sauce over chicken. Top with cheese. Bake 5 minutes uncovered. Makes 4 servings.

MOZZARELLA CHICKEN

1 lb. boneless chicken breast cutlets
1 egg, beaten
Flavored bread crumbs
1 tbsp. olive oil
1 tbsp. margarine
3/4 c. chicken broth
1/4 c. water
3 tbsp. lemon juice
4.8 oz. mozzarella cheese, shredded

Preheat oven to 350 degrees. Dip chicken breast cutlets in egg and coat with bread crumbs. Heat olive oil and margarine in skillet; brown chicken. Place chicken in 9 x 13 inch dish. Combine chicken broth, water and lemon juice. Pour mixture over chicken. Liberally sprinkle cheese over chicken. Bake for 15-20 minutes until cheese melts. Serves 4.

RASPBERRY CHICKEN

4 lb. fryer in pieces
2 c. fresh or frozen raspberries
2 tsp. cornstarch
1/2 c. sugar
1/2 c. cranberry-raspberry cocktail
1/8 tsp. cinnamon
1/8 tsp. allspice
1/8 tsp. nutmeg

Broil chicken in a 9 x 13 inch baking dish to brown and partially cook. Bake at 350 degrees for 30 minutes. Drain the liquid. Cook the rest of the ingredients in a saucepan. Pour over the chicken and cook 1/2 hour more.

CHICKEN AND CRAB VALENTINE

Mix together: 3 c. cooked chicken broken in pieces
2 c. boned crab (2, 4 oz. pkgs.)
8 slices bacon, cooked crisp.

In a double boiler melt 6 tablespoons butter. Stir in 6 tablespoons flour then add the ingredients below.

1 1/2 c. chicken broth
3/4 tsp. paprika
1 sm. clove garlic
5 drops Tabasco
1/8 tsp. nutmeg
1 1/2 tsp. salt

Cover and cook 10-15 minutes stirring often. Add 1 cup sour cream. Mix and heat through. Add chicken, crab and crumbled bacon. Serve with peas and rice tossed with glazed walnuts. To glaze walnuts: Melt in a skillet: 2 tablespoons butter and 2 tablespoons Worcestershire sauce. Add walnuts and stir until walnuts are glazed. Mix with peas and rice.

APRICOT CHICKEN

8 pieces boneless, skinless chicken breasts
1 pkg. onion soup mix
1 (8 oz.) bottle French salad dressing
1 can apricot halves (approximately 16 oz.)

Heat oven to 350 degrees. Mix onion soup, French dressing and juice from apricots. Set aside. Wash chicken breasts and place in an oblong (9 x 13) baking dish. Top chicken with liquid mixture and apricots. Bake for 45 minutes. Serve with rice.

BAKED CHICKEN AND POTATOES

1 fryer chicken, cut up
6 medium unpeeled potatoes, sliced
1 sliced onion
1 can mushroom soup

Put chicken in baking dish and top with potatoes and onion. Add a little water. Bake at 350 degrees for 40 minutes. Add mushroom soup and bake 10 to 20 minutes more.

CHICKEN CRESCENT ALMONDINE

1 (10 3/4 oz.) can condensed cream of chicken soup, undiluted
2/3 c. mayonnaise or salad dressing
1/2 c. sour cream
2 tbsp. instant minced onion
3 c. cooked, cubed chicken
1 (8 oz.) can water chestnuts, drained and sliced
1 (4 oz.) can mushroom stems and pieces, drained
1/2 c. chopped celery
1 (8 oz.) can crescent dinner rolls

--TOPPING--

2/3 c. shredded Swiss or American cheese
1/2 c. slivered almonds
2 tbsp. melted butter

In large saucepan, combine soup, mayonnaise, sour cream and onion. Stir in chicken, water chestnuts, mushrooms and celery; cook over medium heat until mixture is hot and bubbly. Pour into ungreased 13 inch x 9 inch x 2 inch baking dish. Unroll crescent dough and separate into two rectangles, trimming to fit dish. Place dough rectangles over hot chicken mixture.

Combine cheese and almonds; sprinkle over the dough. Drizzle with butter. Bake at 375 degrees for 20-25 minutes or until crust is a deep golden brown. Yield: 8 servings.

CHICKEN AND DUMPLINGS

1 large chicken

Place chicken in stewing kettle with a handful of parsley, a good dash of poultry seasoning and salt and pepper to taste. Simmer 4 hours until tender. Add dumplings to the pot and steam 10 minutes.

--DUMPLINGS--

2 c. flour
4 tsp. baking powder
2/3 c. milk
1/2 tsp. salt
2 tsp. butter

Mix dry ingredients. Work in the butter with finger tips. Add milk gradually. Roll out very thin and cut in strips one inch by two inches. Drop in hot broth.

CHICKEN AND RICE

1 cut-up chicken
1 pkg. herb rice mix (Uncle Ben's long grain wild rice - not instant)
1 can cream of celery soup
1 pkg. onion soup mix
2 soup cans water

Pour dry rice in buttered roasting pan, place chicken parts on top. Sprinkle onion soup mix on top. Mix soup and water, pour over chicken.

Bake 350 degrees for 2 hours. 1/2 hour before done, pour melted butter over chicken.

CHICKEN WITH SAGE CORN - BREAD CRUST

4 skinned and boned chicken thighs
1/8 tsp. salt and pepper
1 tbsp. plus 1 tsp. Dijon mustard
1 tsp. olive oil
2/3 c. corn bread crumbs
1 tbsp. fresh sage, thyme, or rosemary or 1 tsp. each seasoning if you use dried herbs

Preheat oven to 400 degrees. Sprinkle chicken with salt and pepper. Bake 20 to 25 minutes until juices run clear.

In a bowl combine mustard and oil. In another bowl combine crumbs and herbs. Preheat broiler. Set rack 6 inches from heat. Brush half of mustard on chicken and sprinkle on crumbs. Broil until brown, turn chicken and repeat on other side. Serves 4. Calories 178 Saturated fat 1 g. Total fat 7 g. Protein 24 g. Carbohydrate 4 g. Fiber 0 g. Sodium 264 mg. Cholesterol 91 mg.

CHICKEN TERI - YAKI

--TERI SAUCE--

4 c. (1 quart) soy sauce (Kikkoman preferred)
1/4 c. (2 oz.) Mogen David concord white wine or equivalent (optional but it does add special taste - alcohol evaporates when cooking)
1/2 c. (4 oz.) brown sugar
1 oz. garlic powder
1 tsp. of ANI-NO-MOTO or Accent

Cut chicken into serving pieces. Mix above ingredients thoroughly and cook until it boils before cooking chicken. Put chicken into boiling sauce for about 15 minutes. Remove pieces of chicken and broil until brown over charcoal or in oven. Dip again into sauce and broil other side, or just bake in over for about 35 minutes at 325 degrees.

CHINESE STYLE FRIED CHICKEN

2 whole chicken breasts, boned and skinned
2 tomatoes, cut in pieces (1/2 inch)
1 green pepper, cut in pieces (1/2 inch)
2 tbsp. oil
Mushrooms (optional)

--SAUCE--

1/4 c. corn syrup
2 tbsp. soy sauce
1/2 c. water
1 tbsp. corn starch
1/4 tsp. ground ginger
Pinch garlic powder
2 tbsp. sherry (optional)
Mix together

Heat oil in large skillet. Add chicken cut in 1/2 inch pieces and cook for 3 minutes. Stir occasionally. Stir in tomatoes and green pepper. Add sauce, mix, bring to boil, stirring constantly. Continue to boil for 1 minute.

Mixture thickens because of corn starch. Serve over cooked rice Serves 4.

GLAZED ORANGE CHICKEN

No-stick cooking spray
2 tsp. oil
3 whole chicken breasts, halved, skinned and boned
1 tbsp. cornstarch
2 tsp. sugar
1/4 tsp. marjoram
1/8 tsp. salt
1/8 tsp. onion powder
1 1/4 c. unsweetened orange juice
1 tbsp. grated orange peel

Spray large non-stick skillet with cooking spray, add oil. Heat over medium high heat until hot. Cook chicken breasts in hot oil until well browned. In small bowl, combine cornstarch, sugar, marjoram, and salt and onion powder. Gradually stir in orange juice;

stir until well blended. Pour over chicken. Reduce heat, cover and simmer 15 to 20 minutes or until chicken is no longer pink, turning chicken halfway through cooking and stirring occasionally. Sprinkle with orange peel.

HERBED CHICKEN

1 tbsp. olive or vegetable oil
1 medium onion, chopped
1 green or sweet red pepper, chopped
6 lg. fresh mushrooms, thinly sliced
1/3 c. chicken broth
2 tbsp. red wine vinegar
1 (29 oz.) can tomato sauce
2 garlic cloves, minced
1 tsp. sugar
1/4 tsp. salt
1/4 tsp. pepper
1 lb. boneless skinless chicken breasts, cut into chunks
2 tbsp. chopped fresh basil or 1 tsp. dried basil
1 tbsp. chopped fresh sage or 1/2 tsp. dried sage
1 lb. dry linguine, cooked and drained
2 to 3 tbsp. grated Parmesan cheese
2 tbsp. chopped fresh parsley

In a skillet, heat oil over medium high. Saute onion, peppers and mushrooms until tender. Add broth and vinegar; bring to a boil. Boil 2 minutes. Add tomato sauce, garlic, sugar, salt and pepper. Bring to a boil. Reduce heat; cover and simmer 25 minutes. Add chicken, basil and sage.

Cook, uncovered, 15 minutes more or until chicken is done and sauce is lightly thickened. Serve chicken and sauce over pasta. Sprinkle with cheese and parsley. Yield: 4 servings.

ITALIAN CHICKEN CUTLETS

2 whole chicken breasts, skinned, boned, halved
1/4 c. flour
3/4 c. dry bread crumbs
1 tsp. dried oregano leaves
1/4 tsp. salt
1 egg, beaten
1 tbsp. water
1 (8 oz.) can tomato sauce
1/4 tsp. dried basil leaves
1/8 tsp. garlic powder
1/4 c. oil
4 slices (4 oz.) Mozzarella cheese
1/4 c. grated Parmesan cheese

Place 1 chicken breast half, boned side up, between 2 pieces of plastic wrap or waxed paper. Working from center, gently pound chicken with rolling pin or flat side of meat mallet until about 1/4 inch thick. Repeat with remaining chicken pieces, making 4 cutlets. Coat chicken cutlets with flour.

In shallow dish, combine bread crumbs, oregano and salt. In another shallow dish, combine egg and water. Dip each cutlet in egg mixture; coat with crumb mixture. In small saucepan, combine tomato sauce, basil and garlic powder. Cook over low heat until thoroughly heated, stirring occasionally. Meanwhile, heat oil in large skillet over medium high heat until it ripples. Add cutlets; cook until crisp and golden brown on one side, 6 to 8 minutes. Turn; cook other side about 2 minutes or until chicken is no longer pink. Top each cutlet with cheese slice. Cover skillet to melt cheese, about 1 minute.

Place cutlet on serving plate. Serve with sauce and Parmesan cheese. 4 servings.

LIGHT CAPITAL CHICKEN

 2 tbsp. corn oil margarine
4 tbsp. flour
3/4 c. defatted chicken stock
1/2 c. skim milk
1 tbsp. canola oil
3 whole chicken breasts, boned, skinned, split, about 1 1/2 lbs. total
8 oz. fresh mushrooms, sliced, about 3 cups
1 c. each, dry white wine, water
1/2 c. 2% milk

3/4 tsp. salt
1/4 tsp. dried tarragon leaves, crushed
Dash garlic powder
1/4 tsp. freshly ground black pepper
2 tbsp. each, chopped green onions, fresh parsley

Heat oven to 350 degrees. Melt 1 tablespoon of the margarine in medium saucepan. Add 3 tablespoons of flour and stir over medium heat for 1 minute; do not brown. Add chicken stock and skim milk. Using a wire whisk, stir the mixture over medium heat until it comes to a boil.

Continue to cook 1 minute more; set aside. Melt remaining
1 tablespoon margarine in a large skillet along with canola oil. Add chicken and cook over medium heat until brown on both sides, about 5 minutes. Remove chicken and place in baking dish sprayed with non-stick vegetable coating.

Cook mushrooms in same skillet 5 minutes. Stir in remaining 1 tablespoon flour, the sauce, and the wine and water. Simmer, stirring, until thickened about 10 minutes. Stir in 2% milk, salt, tarragon, garlic powder and pepper. Pour over chicken and bake, uncovered until hot (45 minutes). Sprinkle with green onions and parsley; bake 5 minutes.

NO PEEK CHICKEN

1 1/2 c. Minute Rice, uncooked
1 chicken, cut up or pieces
1 pkg. dry onion soup mix
1 can cream of mushroom soup
1 can cream of celery soup

Mix dry rice with mushroom and celery soup. Rinse out cans with a little water and add to mix. Place chicken on top of rice mixture. Sprinkle onion soup on chicken rice mixture. Seal pan completely with tin foil. Bake at 325 degrees for 1 hour. Do not peek or uncover until done.

SKILLET BARBECUED CHICKEN

Chicken, with or without skin, bone or boneless
2 tbsp. butter
1 tsp. curry powder
1 clove garlic, minced
1 can onion soup
2 tbsp. flour
1 1/2 c. of water
1/2 c. of ketchup
1 tbsp. honey
1 tsp. Worcestershire sauce

In large skillet melt butter with curry powder and garlic. Add chicken and brown. Remove chicken. Into drippings, stir soup and flour together. Gradually stir in remaining ingredients. Return chicken to pan. Cover and cook over low heat until chicken is done. About 1 hour. Serve with rice or noodles.

SUNDAY DINNER CHICKEN

8 chicken breasts (boneless and skinless)
1 pkg. chipped beef or 1 jar smoked chipped beef
1 can undiluted cream of chicken soup
1/2 pt. sour cream
(if desired - wrap each piece of chicken with 1 piece of bacon)

Cover bottom of flat, greased baking dish (8x12) with chipped beef. Arrange chicken on top of beef. Mix soup and sour cream. Pour over chicken. Bake at 275 degrees for 3 hours uncovered. Serves 8.

Put into oven when you leave for Sunday School and church. When you get home, cook vegetables, prepare salad and dinner is on the table in 20 minutes.

TARRAGON CHICKEN

2 whole chicken breasts, boned skinned and pounded to 1/4 inch thickness
All purpose flour
4 tbsp. butter, divided
1/2 lb. sliced mushrooms
2 tbsp. all purpose flour
1 c. chicken broth
1 1/4 tsp. minced fresh tarragon or 1/4 tsp. dried tarragon
1/2 c. half and half
Salt and freshly ground black pepper to taste

2-4 Servings. Dredge chicken breasts in flour and brown in 2 tablespoons butter. Remove chicken to warm platter. Add remaining 2 tablespoons butter and saute mushrooms. Sprinkle mushrooms with 2 tablespoons flour, blend well. Gradually add chicken broth, then tarragon, cook until thickened. Slowly add half and half, and season with salt and pepper. Return chicken to pan and heat through. Sauce should be only slightly thick.

TERIYAKI CHICKEN

1 chicken, cut up or 2 lbs. Teriyaki beef or top sirloin steak sliced thin
2 tsp. grated fresh ginger
1 clove garlic, chopped fine
1 medium onion, chopped
1/3 c. soy sauce
1/4 c. sugar
1/4 c. sake

--QUICK TERIYAKI MARINADE--

1 c. soy sauce
1 1/2 - 1 1/4 c. brown sugar
1 tsp. oyster sauce
1 tsp. mirin (sweet rice wine)
1 clove chopped garlic
Grated fresh ginger

Mix all ingredients except meat. Stir and cook over low heat until sugar is dissolved. Cool. Pour over meat and marinate for at least 1 hour. Best when cooked over charcoal. Use remaining marinade for basting.   If you use the Quick Teriyaki

Marinade, mix together and marinate meat for about 1/2 hour. Best when meat is cooked over charcoal. Baste often.

BAKED CHICKEN WINGS

Start with a layer of chicken or turkey wings in a larger roasting pan. Top with 2 cans cream of chicken soup. Then sprinkle with 1 envelope of Lipton onion soup mix.

Then repeat the same two more times. Add 1/2 cup of water and seal with foil paper and bake at 350 degrees for 3 to 4 hours or until tender.

EASY CHICKEN POT PIE

2 c. diced, cooked chicken
1 med. onion, chopped
4 boiled eggs, grated or chopped
2 cans mixed vegetables, drained
2 cans cream of chicken soup
1 can cream of celery soup
1/2 c. chicken broth

--CRUST--

1 c. sweet milk
1 c. mayonnaise
1 c. self-rising flour

Layer first three ingredients in dish. Mix soup, broths and vegetables. Pour over chicken. Mix milk, mayonnaise and flour; spread over soup mix for crust. Bake at 350 degrees for 1 to 1 1/2 hours until golden brown.

TARRAGON CHICKEN

2 whole chicken breasts, boned skinned and pounded to 1/4 inch thickness
All purpose flour
4 tbsp. butter, divided
1/2 lb. sliced mushrooms
2 tbsp. all purpose flour
1 c. chicken broth
1 1/4 tsp. minced fresh tarragon or 1/4 tsp. dried tarragon
1/2 c. half and half
Salt and freshly ground black pepper to taste

2-4 Servings. Dredge chicken breasts in flour and brown in 2 tablespoons butter. Remove chicken to warm platter. Add remaining 2 tablespoons butter and saute mushrooms. Sprinkle mushrooms with 2 tablespoons flour, blend well. Gradually add chicken broth, then tarragon, cook until thickened. Slowly add half and half, and season with salt and pepper. Return chicken to pan and heat through. Sauce should be only slightly thick.

TERIYAKI CHICKEN

1 chicken, cut up or 2 lbs. Teriyaki beef or top sirloin steak sliced thin
2 tsp. grated fresh ginger
1 clove garlic, chopped fine
1 medium onion, chopped
1/3 c. soy sauce
1/4 c. sugar
1/4 c. sake

--QUICK TERIYAKI MARINADE--

1 c. soy sauce
1 1/2 - 1 1/4 c. brown sugar
1 tsp. oyster sauce
1 tsp. mirin (sweet rice wine)
1 clove chopped garlic
Grated fresh ginger

Mix all ingredients except meat. Stir and cook over low heat until sugar is dissolved. Cool. Pour over meat and marinate for at least 1 hour. Best when cooked over charcoal. Use remaining marinade for basting.   If you use the Quick Teriyaki

Marinade, mix together and marinate meat for about 1/2 hour. Best when meat is cooked over charcoal. Baste often.

BAKED CHICKEN WINGS

Start with a layer of chicken or turkey wings in a larger roasting pan. Top with 2 cans cream of chicken soup. Then sprinkle with 1 envelope of Lipton onion soup mix.

Then repeat the same two more times. Add 1/2 cup of water and seal with foil paper and bake at 350 degrees for 3 to 4 hours or until tender.

EASY CHICKEN POT PIE

2 c. diced, cooked chicken
1 med. onion, chopped
4 boiled eggs, grated or chopped
2 cans mixed vegetables, drained
2 cans cream of chicken soup
1 can cream of celery soup
1/2 c. chicken broth

--CRUST--

1 c. sweet milk
1 c. mayonnaise
1 c. self-rising flour

Layer first three ingredients in dish. Mix soup, broths and vegetables. Pour over chicken. Mix milk, mayonnaise and flour; spread over soup mix for crust. Bake at 350 degrees for 1 to 1 1/2 hours until golden brown.

CHICKEN DELIGHT

15-20 cut up chicken pieces
1 can cream of chicken soup
1 can cream of celery soup
1 green bell pepper
1 red or yellow pepper
1 can water

Wash chicken. Season with pepper and your favorite seasoning salt. (I like McCormick's.) Refrigerate chicken overnight allowing seasonings to soak throughout. Cut peppers into slices and set aside.

Mix soups and water in bowl. Add peppers and pour over chicken. Bake at 350 degrees for about 1 hour and 15 minutes.

NOTE: The broth from this dish may be used as gravy for dressing.

CHICKEN A LA KING

2 tablespoons fat
2 tablespoons flour
1 cup milk
1 cup cream
2 egg yolks
1 green pepper, minced
1 cup quartered mushrooms
1 pimiento cut in narrow strips
2 cups cooked diced chicken
1 teaspoon salt
1/2 teaspoon pepper

Make a white sauce using meat drippings, flour, milk, cream, salt and pepper. Add mushrooms, green pepper, pimiento and chicken. Cook until the meat is done. Just before serving stir in the egg yolks, slightly beaten, and cook for a about a minute or two, stirring constantly. Serve at once on hot toast

www.ingramcontent.com/pod-product-compliance
Lightning Source LLC
Chambersburg PA
CBHW081618100526
44590CB00021B/3495